New Testament Ethics
The Story Retold

the *1997*

J.J. THIESSEN LECTURES

New Testament Ethics
The Story Retold

by

RICHARD B. HAYS

WIPF *&* STOCK · Eugene, Oregon

Wipf and Stock Publishers
199 W 8th Ave, Suite 3
Eugene, OR 97401

New Testament Ethics
The Story Retold
By Hays, Richard B.
Copyright©1998 Canadian Mennonite University Press
ISBN 13: 978-1-5326-5763-4
Publication date 5/14/2018
Previously published by Canadian Mennonite University Press, 1998

CONTENTS

The 1997 J.J. Thiessen Lectures
were presented at
Canadian Mennonite Bible College
on October 21–22, 1997

Portions of these lectures are adapted from Richard B. Hays, *The Moral Vision of the New Testament: Community, Cross, New Creation* (San Francisco, California: HarperSanFrancisco, 1996) and reprinted here by permission.

FOREWORD

Every year in October the community at Canadian Mennonite Bible College adjusts its normal routine for two days to hear a prominent scholar on a topic pertinent to the college's program of studies. This event brings together not only the students of the college but also church leaders and scholars from the local community. These are important days.

The lectures are named in honour of a Canadian Mennonite churchman—Rev. J.J. Thiessen—who believed in the importance of the kind of Christian education that inspired people to faithful Christian living. His life expressed the conviction that the truth of theology could not be spoken once for always, but that the time and place of its living required fresh embrace and renewed ownership. Hence his love for Christian education. And for him this love was intimately connected with a cultivated memory, not only of the story of faith but of the names of the people who comprise the community of faith.

In 1997 Professor Richard Hays delivered the J.J. Thiessen Lectures on the topic, "New Testament Ethics: The Story Retold." In these lectures, as in his writings, Hays' passion for getting the story right and his conviction that Christians today are part of that story, become apparent. He has taught us that our "getting it right" has to do not only with intellectual interests and rigour, but with the truthful practices of today's Christians.

We are pleased that these lectures are here made available to a larger audience. We thank Professor Hays for accepting our invitation, for presenting the lectures, and for the additional work that is required to make out of a good lecture a good essay.

Harry Huebner
Chair of CMBC Lectureship Committee
October 1998

Richard B. Hays, Professor of New Testament at Duke Divinity School, Durham, North Carolina, since 1991, is an ordained United Methodist minister. He received his B.A. and M.Div. Degrees from Yale University and his Ph.D. from Emory University in Atlanta, where he taught in the Chandler School of Theology. He also taught at Yale Divinity School for ten years. Hays is noted for his work in the field of Pauline theology and New Testament ethics. His books include: *The Moral Vision of the New Testament: Community, Cross, New Creation* (Harper SanFrancisco, 1996), *Echoes of Scripture in the Letters of Paul* (Yale University Press, 1989) and *First Corinthians* (*Interpretation* commentary series; John Knox Press, 1997).

1
MAPPING THE FIELD
APPROACHES TO NEW TESTAMENT ETHICS

New Testament Ethics as a Problem

"The Devil can cite Scripture to his purpose," so my grandmother used to say. Or, as we prefer to say now in the academy, "The text has inexhaustible hermeneutical potential." No matter how we choose to phrase it, the problem is the same. Despite the time-honored Christian claim that Scripture is the source and foundation for the church's faith and practice, it is not easy to see how Scripture can direct our speech and action, given the seemingly endless diversity of *readings* of Scripture.

Our difficulty is nowhere more evident than with regard to ethical questions. I offer you just one example drawn from recent political controversy in the United States to illustrate the problem. After Bill Clinton's victory in the 1992 presidential election, some conservative Christians—defenders of what they claimed to be biblical "family values"—were scandalized by the Rev. Billy Graham's decision to participate in the inaugural festivities. They drafted a letter of protest asking Graham not to pray for Clinton. "Bill Clinton ran for office as an outspoken advocate of abortion on demand and legitimized homosexuality," they wrote. "Of course, we realize that other presidents have been endorsed by church leaders who might not have held biblical positions on all issues [*sic*],[1] but never in recent history has a presidential candidate with such an explicitly *unbiblical* platform been elected to our nation's highest office."[2] Graham, undeterred by this protest, did participate in the inauguration, where he heard Clinton bring his inaugural address to its climax by quoting Galatians 6:9: "Let us not be weary in well-doing, for in due season we shall reap, if we faint not."

Such uses of biblical language in political rhetoric exemplify a perennial difficulty: everybody wants to claim the Bible. Christians of all sorts, even those who might not subscribe formally to a "high" doctrine of biblical inspiration, have always deemed it essential that their ethical teachings and practices stand in continuity with Scripture.[3]

In light of such profound disagreements about the message—or application—of Scripture, an outsider's skepticism might be understandable: when Christians appeal to the Bible as the basis of morality, is such an appeal anything more than rhetorical posturing? The dilemma is most poignant, however, when seen from within the community of faith: how can the church become a Scripture-shaped community, even where it earnestly longs to do so? Those who can naively affirm the bumper-sticker slogan, "God said it, I believe it, that settles it," are oblivious to the question-begging inherent in the formulation: there is no escape from the imperative of interpreting the word. Bumper-sticker hermeneutics will not do.

Unless we can give a coherent account of how we move between the biblical text and normative ethical judgments, appeals to the authority of Scripture will be hollow and unconvincing. Is there such a thing as New Testament ethics? How can the church read Scripture in a faithful and disciplined manner so that Scripture might come to shape the life of the community?

In my book, *The Moral Vision of the New Testament*,[4] I have proposed some answers to these problems, but the answers I offer there are far from definitive or uncontroversial. Indeed, even the way I have defined the problem in these opening remarks would be strongly contested by others working in this field. What I propose to do in this series of lectures is to place my approach to New Testament ethics in the context of some other current approaches and to develop my own reflections somewhat more fully in response to certain challenges that have emerged since the publication of the book a year ago.

The outline of the four lectures will be as follows: (1) In the first, I will map the field by describing broadly some of the differing ways in which theologians and New Testament scholars have sought to bring the study of the New Testament into conversation with the discipline of Christian ethics. (2) In the second lecture I will summarize my own approach and develop some fresh reflections about how my project is related to the "Rule of Faith" and the confessional traditions of the church. (3) In the third lecture, I will take up the question of the significance of the historical Jesus for New Testament ethics, engaging particularly in conversation with some of the recent work of Luke Timothy Johnson and N. T. Wright. (4) Finally, I will address the issue of the New Testament's teaching about the relation between men and women in the church—a matter that I skirted in *Moral Vision of the New Testament*. By taking up this new topic, I hope to offer further illustrations of how my proposed method of New Testament ethics as "metaphor-making" works out in practice.

Mapping the Field

In the spring of 1995, a major conference was held at Duke University under the sponsorship of a grant that I received from the Pew Charitable Trusts. Its topic was: "The New Testament and Ethics: Problems and Prospects." The conference brought together about 30 leading New Testament scholars, theologians, and ethicists to discuss ways in which their disciplines might be brought together fruitfully. The roster of participants included New Testament scholars such as Wayne Meeks, Elisabeth Schüssler Fiorenza, Leander Keck, Victor Furnish, Luke Timothy Johnson, and N. T. Wright. Among the theologians who participated were Nicholas Lash, Stanley Hauerwas, George Lindbeck, Rowan Williams, L. Gregory Jones, Oliver O'Donovan, and John Howard Yoder. The conference was structured around discussions of five books either recently published or then still in manuscript form: Wayne A. Meeks,

The Origins of Christian Morality;[5] Elisabeth Schüssler-Fiorenza, *But She Said;*[6] Oliver O'Donovan, *The Desire of the Nations;*[7] Richard B. Hays, *The Moral Vision of the New Testament;* and Ellen T. Charry, *By the Renewing of Your Minds: The Pastoral Function of Christian Doctrine.*[8] We were attempting to ask how each of these books addressed the relationship between the New Testament and ethics. What methods are to be employed? How can we move from exegetical work to the formation of normative moral judgments? Or is such a move possible? If so, what sort of norms would emerge from the critical process?

I regret to report that the conference was spectacularly unsuccessful—at least if "success" is defined as the achievement of consensus. Indeed, although we had originally intended to publish the papers from the conference, in the end we decided against it, because much of the discussion was so acrimonious and unfruitful. In many of the sessions, we found it almost impossible to agree on either the appropriate subject matter or the appropriate method for such a conversation. So, despite (or *because of?*) the presence of so many outstanding scholars with stimulating ideas and deep concern for bringing New Testament study together with ethical reflection, we found ourselves talking at cross purposes and ending in confusion and frustration. In my gloomiest and more melodramatic moments at the end of conference, I found myself feeling like the speaker in Matthew Arnold's poem "Dover Beach," who hears "the Sea of Faith" retreating and looks around, lamenting:

> And we are here as on a darkling plain
> Swept with confused alarms of struggle and flight,
> Where ignorant armies clash by night.

Is there a way forward from this impasse? Before we can begin to move forward, we need to survey the battlefield. (In present company, I hate to use the military metaphor, but it seems unavoidable under the circumstances.) We need to map the terrain of the recent discussion to see how the opposing forces are positioned—and perhaps also in the process discover where some of the land mines might be buried.

I propose that recent treatments of "the New Testament and ethics" can be categorized into six distinguishable groups. (I will not call them "batallions;" perhaps we should think of them as "schools of thought" or, better yet, "models.") Each of these models represents a particular conception of how the study of ethics is to be related to the New Testament. This six-fold typology is perhaps a little artificial, for individual inter-preters may sometimes employ the methods of more than one of these models. Nonetheless, I think the categories are useful for helping us sort out what is happening in the clash of argument and counter argument. In each case, we are asking the following questions: (1) How is the subject matter of New Testament ethics to be defined? (2) What is the relationship between exegesis and normative ethical judgment? (3) What normative significance is to be given to the New Testament canon? (4) By whom and for whom is the work of critical reflection on the relation between New Testament and ethics being done?

Historical Description of the Ethical Teaching of the New Testament Writings. Most books on New Testament ethics by New Testament scholars have fallen into this category. Wolf-gang Schrage's book *The Ethics of the New Testament,* a widely-used text, exemplifies this approach.[9] Schrage begins with a lengthy historical reconstruction of the ethical teachings of Jesus. This is followed by a short chapter on "Ethical Beginnings in the Earliest Congregations"—i.e., on the fragmentary pre-synoptic and pre-Pauline traditions that can be recovered by form-critical analysis of the canonical texts—then another brief chapter on "Ethical Accents in the Synoptic Gospels." The latter chapter gives very brief discussions of the distinctive "spin" given to the Jesus tradition by each of the synoptic evangelists. Another lengthy chapter on Paul's ethics is followed by separate chapters on the deutero-Pauline epistles, James, the Johannine writings, Hebrews, and Revelation. The overall schema aims at providing a picture of historical development, beginning with Jesus and tracing subsequent developments. There is no treatment of extracanonical writings, so the New Testament canon is treated as a self-contained entity.

Nonetheless, Schrage insists that "[t]here is no such thing as the ethics of *the* New Testament." Rather, "[t]he proper methodology is to see that each individual voice is heard, so that the various early Christian models are not forced into a single mold or submerged into an imaginary New Testament ethics."[10] Thus, despite a consistent emphasis on "the law of love" as the guiding factor in the New Testament, Schrage's book contains no synthetic reflection about the unity of the New Testament canon as ethical witness.[11] Nor does Schrage attempt to relate his discussion specifically to the formation of normative ethical judgments for our time. Schrage certainly believes that the New Testament is relevant to such judgments, and one finds scattered throughout the book statements that assume the New Testament's claim on our lives. The point is, however, that Schrage is content to define his project as one of historical description of the New Testament's teaching. The development of normative judgment is left to the readers: presumably it is the province of theologians, ethicists, and pastors. This division of labor between the "biblical scholar" as historian and the "theologian" who does the subsequent normative work has characterized the academic study of theology since the Enlightenment. In my judgment, this division has led to a disastrous bifurcation of discourse that has made it difficult for theologians and biblical scholars even to talk to each other. That is part of the problem that we experienced in the conference at Duke.

One more point needs to be noted about Schrage's work: he

is concerned to describe the ethical ideas and teachings of the New Testament rather than to examine the actual practices of the early Christians. This is made explicit in his introduction: "The primary subject of our study will . . . not be the practical realization of ethical principles, the early Christian ethos, but the theological motivation and justification of New Testament ethics, its basic criteria and concrete requirements."[12] Thus, his treatment of New Testament ethics is a subfield within the larger area of New Testament theology.

Frank Matera's recent book, *New Testament Ethics: The Legacies of Jesus and Paul*[13] belongs within this same category. Matera, however, gives less attention than Schrage to developmental history (for example, he does not try to reconstruct the teachings of Jesus), and he gives more attention to the distinctive profile of the ethical teaching of each of the canonical gospels.

Ethnographic Description of the Social World of the Early Christians. Schrage's focus on theology stands in sharp contrast to the work of Wayne Meeks, the leading figure of a group of New Testament scholars who have come to see themselves primarily as social historians of the early Christian movement. Meeks eschews theological analysis, and he is far more interested in how the early Christians actually lived than in what they thought. Their thought is important because it constructed a symbolic world within which they acted, but the really interesting thing about the New Testament is the way in which it provides a window onto the social reality of the early Christian communities. According to this moder, the New Testament scholar is like an anthropologist seeking to "visit" ancient communities in the Mediterranean world and to offer an ethnographic account, a "thick description" of their life and practices.[14] Meeks's magisterial book, *The First Urban Christians,*[15] worked out this program in detail for the Pauline churches, and he has subsequently written two books that deal more broadly with issues that intersect New Testament ethics: *The Moral World of the First Christians*[16] and *The Origins of Christian Morality*. Meeks prefers to speak of "morality" rather than "ethics," because the latter term implies systematic normative reflection, whereas the former can be used more broadly to describe the codes of behavior that govern—or characterize—daily life. "Morality" may or may not be fully thought through; it is "a pervasive and, often, only partly conscious set of value-laden dispositions, inclinations, and habits."[17] In Meeks's judgment, this is a better term to characterize the operative norms in the early Christian communities.

Furthermore, Meeks does not want to confine his attention to the New Testament canon. As a social historian, he is interested in all evidence that can shed light on the social structure and experience of early Christian communities. Thus, in *The Moral World of the First Christians,* he spends the first half of the book investigating the world of the Greek *polis* within the Roman Empire and outlining the salient features of moral teaching traditions in Greco-Roman philosophy and Jewish tradition. He then looks at selected New Testament documents but gives equal attention to the *Didache* and to the writings of Irenaeus. In this respect, of course, Meeks stands within a well established tradition of New Testament scholarship: the *religionsgeschichtliche Schule* in German biblical scholarship at the end of the nineteenth century had insisted on placing the study of the New Testament within the framework of Hellenistic religion and philosophy, and attending to the *religion* of the early Christians rather than merely the ideational content of their theology. Indeed, in several respects, Meeks's work carries forward the program outlined by William Wrede in his 1897 essay entitled, "The Task and Methods of New Theology."[18]

In view of all this, it probably goes without saying that Meeks shies away from translating the results of his studies into normative ethical reflections. His ethnography of ancient

communities is designed as a purely *wissenschaftlich* enterprise, taking its place in the secular university alongside other
purportedly value-neutral investigations in the humanities and
social sciences. One result of his studies is to heighten our
awareness of the great cultural and historical distance between
our world and the ancient Mediterranean world. To appropriate
early Christian texts in a direct way as normative for today is
highly dubious and even dangerous. In his most recent major
book, *The Origins of Christian Morality,* he writes: "The
purpose of this inquiry has been resolutely historical and
descriptive. It will have succeeded to a large extent if it has
done no more than to make the ethos of the early Christians
seem even more distant from the ordinary concerns and beliefs
of people today than it did before."[19] Nonetheless, he does offer
in the conclusion of the book seven "Preliminary Theses on
Christian Morality" that might be of some help in thinking
about "the state of Christian moral discourse today."

These theses remain at a high level of generality, primarily
emphasizing the difficulty of reaching determinate moral
judgments. There is not time in this lecture to discuss them, but
I will enumerate them so that you can get a sense for the
character of the guidance that Meeks offers us as the fruit of his
work on early Christian communities: (1) Making morals and
making community are one, dialectical process. (2) A Christian
moral community must be grounded in the past. (3) The
church's rootage in Israel is a privileged dimension of its past.
(4) Faithfulness ought not be confused with nostalgia. (5)
Christian ethics must be polyphonic. (6) Moral confidence, not
moral certainty, is what we require. (7) God tends to surprise.[20]

Unfortunately, Meeks has so far left us in the dark about the
specific shape of the Christian community that he believes
desirable for our time and about the specific shape of the moral
life in which we are supposed to have "moral confidence." In
this respect, Meeks, along with most other exponents of this
ethnographic approach, shares with the first model a willing-

ness to restrict the work of the New Testament scholar to the purely descriptive level. As long as one thinks of the university as one's primary audience, this is understandable. However, when the correlation of New Testament and ethics arises as an issue for the *church,* it is impossible to defer normative questions indefinitely. We must decide how to order our communities in response to the Word. I turn, therefore, to consider other models that do include normative deliberation as part of the task of correlating ethics and the New Testament.

Extraction of Ideals or Principles. This approach is very widespread, both among ethicists and in much popular preaching and piety—though it is decidedly out of favor with most New Testament scholars. In this model, the stories and letters of the New Testament are taken as carriers of a moral message that can and must be extracted from them, in the form of ideals, principles, or ethical themes, such as love, justice, or liberation. The New Testament texts serve as boxcars that carry the freight of these general moral concepts. It is characteristic of this approach that once the freight is delivered, once we have the concept, we no longer really need the story. In Part III of *Moral Vision of the New Testament,* I offer an analysis of the use of Scripture by several theological ethicists. Of the figures I discuss there, Reinhold Niebuhr most clearly exemplifies this model.[21] Niebuhr treats the love-ethic of Jesus as an "impossible ideal" that cannot be practiced directly by human beings. It can only be approximated through the attempt to enforce the principle of justice in human societies, which will require the use of violence because of the pervasive reality of human sinfulness. Thus, Niebuhr's appeal to the "ideal" of love and the principle of justice allows him to overturn the normative force of Jesus' explicit teaching against violence in the Sermon on the Mount. Niebuhr follows Augustine in believing that responsible Christians may have to do violence in the cause of justice.

This approach of course makes it much easier to bridge the hermeneutical gap between the world of the New Testament and our world, but it does so by constructing an ethic that is abstracted away from the specific commands, rules, and stories of the Bible. Interpreters who work in this model often pay relatively little attention to detailed exegesis and ignore the shape and content of the biblical narratives. The New Testament is used in a highly selective way, as the interpreter lifts out nuggets of truth and ignores the rest. This is particularly clear in Niebuhr's work, but one sees similar tendencies in some texts on New Testament ethics, such as Eduard Lohse's *Theological Ethics of the New Testament*[22] or Ceslas Spicq's *Theologie Morale du Nouveau Testament*. Likewise, in the work of some liberation theologians, one sometimes senses that a particular theme or principle, such as liberation or justice, has become an independent construct no longer governed by the biblical narratives. The New Testament texts become illustrative material for moral claims that can equally well be articulated in other languages, such as the Enlightenment ideal of "human rights." Scripture may stand in the background as the ultimate source of the ideals that inform moral judgment, but its relation to specific decisions and actions is distant and indirect. In effect, the Bible's explicit moral teachings and demands are replaced by a process of "realistic" consequentialist calculation. (This is not necessarily true of all liberation theologians or of all interpreters who highlight principles as the key to using the New Testament in normative ethics but this is a hazard built in to this model.) It is noteworthy that Niebuhr writes as a public theologian addressing individual readers in a democratic society. He assumes that his audience is made up of Christians, but he has no discernible ecclesiology. In effect, his ethic speaks to individuals and governments, but leaves the church out of account. He has no vision of the church as a prophetic counterculture; instead, he assumes that Christians must be "responsible" for managing the politics of a secular world.

Cultural Critique of Ideologies in the New Testament. Within the past 15 or 20 years, we have seen the rise of a new phenomenon: interpreters who understand themselves to be Christian theologians and biblical scholars have begun to apply a "hermeneutics of suspicion" to Scripture. The claim is made that the Bible contains various ideologies—notably patriarchy—that are fundamentally destructive of human wholeness. In such works, the apostolic witnesses are sometimes portrayed less as revelatory witnesses to God's mercy than as oppressive promulgators of abusive images of God. For example, Elisabeth Schüssler Fiorenza, the leading feminist New Testament scholar, writes, ". . . a feminist critical hermeneutics of suspicion places a warning label on all biblical texts: *Caution! Could be dangerous to your health and survival.*"[23] This does not mean that the Bible is categorically rejected by such interpreters; it can contain liberating as well as oppressive messages. Nonetheless, it must be subjected to ideological critique. Elsewhere, Schüssler Fiorenza explains:

> [N]o biblical patriarchal text that perpetuates violence against women, children, or "slaves" should be accorded the status of divine revelation if we do not want to turn the God of the Bible into a God of violence. That does not mean that we cannot preach . . . on the household code texts of the New Testament. It only means that we must preach them critically in order to unmask them as texts promoting patriarchal violence.[24]

The moral passion of such statements is to be welcomed. Sadly, our common history does bear witness to epidemic violence, including violence against women, children, and the powerless. Certainly this violence is to be condemned, and one might hope that interpreters of the Bible would have good grounds for proclaiming such condemnation. The difficulty in which we find ourselves, however, is this: if the Bible itself—the revelatory, identity-defining text of the Christian community—contains texts that authorize and promote such violence, what are we to do? What is the ground on which we stand to conduct a critique of Scripture? For Schüssler Fiorenza, the answer is clear: a feminist critical hermeneutic "does not appeal to the Bible as its primary source but begins with women's own experience and vision of liberation."[25] *Experience* (of a certain sort) is treated as unambiguously revelatory, and the Bible is critically scrutinized in its light.

One way of putting this point is to say that interpreters within this model begin with some sort of intuitive or experientially-based knowledge of "ethics," then use this knowledge as a critical grid against which biblical texts must be measured. This would be an overly simplified account of the matter, because, as Schüssler Fiorenza insists, the Bible is the source of women's power as well as of their oppression.[26] What is needed, she proposes, is a "feminist critical hermeneutic of liberation" that will retrieve liberating traditions buried in the biblical texts and, at the same time, critically challenge oppressive ideologies found within these same texts.

In this respect, Schüssler Fiorenza's work may be seen as a development of Rudolph Bultmann's demythologizing hermeneutic, which sought to discern the existential meaning expressed by the New Testament texts and then in turn to critique the inadequate language and images through which that message was brought to expression by the various New Testament writers. The German term for this sort of criticism is *Sachkritik,* which is hard to translate into English. It means something like "criticism on the basis of the substance" of a text. [For a classically Bultmannian outworking of an approach to New Testament ethics along these lines, see Willi Marxsen, *New Testament Foundations for Christian Ethics.*[27]] The thing that is new in the work of feminist critics—as well as others who employ similar methodologies, such as gay liberationists, and advocates of other oppressed groups—is that they explicitly begin with a particular *social* or *political* advocacy stance and use this as a programmatic basis for evaluating the ethical impact of all biblical texts. Where the texts fail to pass this ideological screening mechanism, they are to be "unmasked" and subjected to critical scrutiny.

It will be evident to you that this sort of ideological criticism manifests none of the hesitation that we saw in the first two models about making normative ethical judgments. Indeed, the practitioners of this cultural criticism insist that all interpretations are "interested," and that the pose of "objectivity" in older biblical scholarship was merely a rhetorical ruse that concealed the hegemony of the white male patriarchal system. There is no such thing as a "purely descriptive" exegesis of a New Testament text, because every description has ethical consequences and either empowers or disempowers someone.

At its best, this approach to the New Testament renders a powerful reading of the early Christian community as a community of equals living in the power and love of the Holy Spirit, challenging the oppressive social conventions of their time and offering a compelling prototype for our own efforts to create a more just community.

The obvious difficulty with this model is that it tends, even more drastically than the previous model, to diminish any meaningful claim for the authority of the New Testament. It decides in advance what must be true. Schüssler Fiorenza draws the logical conclusion from all this:

> . . . the revelatory canon for theological evaluation of biblical androcentric traditions . . . cannot be derived from the Bible itself but can only be formulated in and through women's struggle for liberation from all patriarchal oppression. . . . The personally and politically reflected experience of oppression and liberation must become the criterion of appropriateness for biblical interpretation and evaluation of biblical authority claims.[28]

In this schema, the Bible has become the norma normata, and

it may serve merely as illustrative material for ethical convictions held independently on other grounds.

Character-Formation and "the Ethics of Reading." The fifth model for your consideration is exemplified by my colleague at Duke, Stanley Hauerwas, who has championed an approach to ethics that emphasizes the formation of character—in contrast to conceptions of ethics that stress rules, principles, and decisions. He is concerned not so much with defining moral action as with the formation of the moral agent. Hauerwas is not a New Testament scholar, but he is concerned to show that the biblical narratives have the effect of shaping what he calls "a community of character," a body of people taught by God's grace to live in nonviolence and forgiveness.

In contrast to approaches that try first to derive an ethic from the New Testament and then to use it to guide the moral life, Hauerwas characteristically puts the matter the other way around: the church must be a truthful and peaceable community in order to be able to read the New Testament's portrayal of Jesus rightly. This may appear to be a chicken-and-egg paradox, but Hauerwas insists that the epistemological issue is real and crucial. He prefaces a telling quotation from Athanasius to his essay "Jesus: The Story of the Kingdom:"

> For the searching and right understanding of the Scriptures there is need of a good life and a pure soul, and for Christian virtue to guide the mind to grasp, so far as human nature can, the truth concerning God the Word. One cannot possibly understand the teaching of the saints unless one has a pure mind and is trying to imitate their life. . . . [A]nyone who wishes to understand the mind of the sacred writers must first cleanse his own life, and approach the saints by copying their deeds.[29]

Thus, obedience must precede understanding. Athanasius formulates this hermeneutical dictum in terms of the character of the individual interpreter, but Hauerwas extends Athanasius' logic to the character of the church as an interpretive community. The most important task of the church is "to be a community *capable of hearing* the story of God we find in the scripture and living in a manner that is faithful to that story."[30] If and only if we are such a community can we seek to derive moral guidance from the story of Jesus. (For example, Hauerwas contends that you have to be a pacifist in order to read the Sermon on the Mount rightly.) Readings of Scripture that occur outside the context of the church as a character-forming community will merely underwrite "the ideology of a politics quite different from the politics of the church;"[31] in other words, such readings will promote individualism, self-indulgence, and violence. The extent to which Hauerwas is willing to press this methodological point is revealed in the opening paragraph of *Unleashing the Scripture:*

> Most North American Christians assume they have a right, if not an obligation, to read the Bible. I challenge that assumption. No task is more important than for the church to take the Bible out of the hands of individual Christians in North America. Let us no longer give the Bible to every child when they enter the third grade or whenever their assumed rise to Christian maturity is marked. . . . Let us rather tell them and their parents that they are possessed by habits far too corrupt for them to be encouraged to read the Bible on their own.[32]

Only a community already formed by the story of the Kingdom of God can begin to read Scripture rightly.

How does that formation occur? Through the example of the lives of the saints (by which Hauerwas means all our fathers and mothers in the faith) and through the church's liturgy, especially the Eucharist. For Hauerwas, the Lord's Supper is a community-forming tradition that creates the indispensable context for the interpretation of Scripture. Thus, for him, there is no "problem" about how to relate ethics and the New Testament. We are embedded already in a community, the church, whose traditions teach us how to read the story of Jesus. As we participate in that community, we are shaped by that story to become a peaceful people, forgiven and forgiving. His constant concern, then, is not for rigorous methods of interpretation, but rather for the character of the community

Another widely read recent work that takes a similar approach is the book, *Reading in Communion* by Stephen Fowl and L. Gregory Jones.[33] They seek to show how we can become "wise readers of Scripture," and they offer extended accounts of particular figures, such as Dietrich Bonhoeffer, who exemplify authentic reading and "performing" of Scripture.

Under the heading of this model, we might also group those works that concern themselves with the "ethics of reading." A significant recent example is Daniel Patte's book, *Ethics of Biblical Interpretation: A Reevaluation*.[34] Patte's theoretical framework is vastly different from that of Hauerwas, Fowl, and Jones, but he shares the focus on the ethical formation of the interpreter as the central issue to be addressed when we consider the relationship between Bible and ethics. Patte is particularly concerned to urge white male historical critics to become "ethically responsible" interpreters by acknowledging their own privileged social location and becoming "androcritical" readers of the New Testament.

I will not take the time here to detail a critique of this approach. (See *Moral Vision*, 253–266, for my treatment of Hauerwas.) The biggest difficulty with it is that, like model 4 above, it fails to explain how the New Testament can ever serve as a critical norm in judgment of the community at times when the church becomes unfaithful, for according to Hauerwas's account, "the church creates the meaning of Scripture."[35] Such reader-centered approaches threaten to deprive the New Testament witnesses of any voice that can challenge or correct us. Furthermore, even if one grants the theoretical premises of

Hauerwas's program, we are still left with the problem of how to describe the message we receive from Scripture when it is read within the community of faith. Hauerwas rarely attends to specific exegetical problems, nor does he wrestle with the problem of what to do when teachings within the New Testament canon stand in tension with one another. But these are precisely the problems that New Testament ethics must contend with. Thus, in one sense Hauerwas leaves us back where we started: how are we to read *these texts* and correlate them with the ethical issues that we confront in our time?

Metaphorical Embodiment of Narrative Paradigms. The final model that I want to propose as a possible way of construing the relation between ethics and the New Testament is—no surprise—my own. (You've known this was coming all along: teachers always save the solution to the problem for the end.) When I say it is my own, I do not mean that I invented it or that it is unprecedented. Indeed, the approach I developed in *The Moral Vision of the New Testament* has deep affinities with the theology and ethics of Karl Barth and John Howard Yoder, and with the theology of the so-called "Yale School," which took its inspiration particularly from the work of Hans Frei.

I will outline my approach in much more detail in the second lecture, so I will be brief for now. The defining characteristic of this sixth model for relating Scripture and ethics is that it reads the Bible as a *story* that narrates God's gracious action for the reconciliation of the world. This story creates a symbolic world in which we are to find our orientation and identity. Another term for this story is, simply, "the gospel." The task of ethical discernment then becomes to discern and create metaphorical correspondences between our communities in the present and the communities whose story is told in the New Testament, so that the gospel story continues in our midst. In this model, the stories of the New Testament canon are privileged. We do not stand in judgment over them; rather, they confront and form and shape us. (This emphasis on the priority of the canonical narratives distinguishes model 6 from models 3, 4, and 5. Hauerwas [model 5] also emphasizes narrative, but he subordinates Scripture to the church, rather than vice-versa.)

Our first business, then, is to listen as carefully to the New Testament witnesses as possible. This is a complex task, because the New Testament is not a homogeneous book. There are distinct voices in it. We must learn to hear these voices and to understand their complex polyphonic relation to one another. Thus, careful critical exegesis is essential to this model.

But this model does not stop with descriptive exegesis. Right understanding of the texts is possible only when we act in obedience to them. Thus, the move from the descriptive work of reading the texts to the normative work of deciding and acting is an essential component of New Testament ethics. (In this respect, model 6 agrees with models 4 and 5). This is not a business for dispassionate critics or mildly curious spectators. Rather, New Testament ethics requires a confessional, self-involving commitment to put what we read into practice.

Summary and Outlook

I am aware that I have merely given you a teaser here. Particularly with regard to model 6, I have offered no more than a preview of the second lecture. But I hope that this sketchy mapping of the field is of some help in providing an orientation to the issues in the hotly contested battle over New Testament ethics. The six models that I have outlined have different strengths and weaknesses. I would certainly want to emphasize that I have learned important things from all of them. The first two models, which restrict themselves to the descriptive task of New Testament interpretation, have given rise to numerous careful studies that greatly enhance our understanding of the New Testament and its historical setting. The third and fourth models in different ways pose sharply the challenge of hermeneutics: how can we hear these texts as relevant to our world, and how do we deal with the acute tensions between the ancient world and our own? The fifth model helps us recognize our dependence on tradition and community and focuses attention on the moral qualities that we as readers bring to the texts. And the sixth model asserts Scripture's claim on us as the word of God, while reckoning seriously with its diversity and narrative form. I hope this map of the battlefield will help you to negotiate your way around this "darkling plain"—or at least the part of it where academic armies clash over the territory of New Testament ethics.

Notes

1. One assumes that the writers meant to say ". . . church leaders have endorsed other presidents who might not have held biblical positions on all issues."

2. Patrick Mahoney and Bill Devlin as quoted in *The Christian Century*, 101 (January 20, 1993): 49.

3. For a case study approach that shows how the Bible has been used to support conflicting positions on controversial issues, see Willard Swartley *Slavery, Sabbath, War, and Women: Case Studies in Biblical Interpretation* (Louisville: Westminster/John Knox, 1983).

4. Richard B. Hays, *The Moral Vision of the New Testament: Community, Cross, New Creation: A Contemporary Introduction to New Testament Ethics* (San Francisco: Harper San Francisco, 1996).

5. Wayne A. Meeks, *The Origins of Christian Morality: The First Two Centuries* (New Haven: Yale University Press, 1993).

6. Elisabeth Schüssler Fiorenza, *But She Said: Feminist Practices of Biblical Interpretation* (Boston: Beacon Press, 1992).

7. Oliver O'Donovan, *The Desire of the Nations: Rediscovering the Roots of Political Theology* (New York: Cambridge University Press, 1996).

8. Ellen T. Charry, *By the Renewing of Your Minds: The Pastoral Function of Christian Doctrine* (New York: Oxford University Press, 1997).

9. Wolfgang Schrage, *The Ethics of the New Testament*, trans. David E. Green (Philadelphia: Fortress Press, 1988).

10. Ibid., 3.

11. In the introduction (page 8), Schrage does assert that Jesus, the Synoptics, Paul, and John share a common "theological or christological foundation;" consequently, he is able to say that "New Testament ethics is neither autonomous nor teleological. Its criterion and basis is God's saving act in Jesus Christ." This assertion is supported by his treatment of the individual "voices," but it is never developed programmatically in the book as the basis for a synthesis.

12. Schrage, *Ethics of the New Testament,* 4.

13. Frank J. Matera, *New Testament Ethics: The Legacies of Jesus and Paul* (Louisville: Westminster John Knox, 1996).

14. Meeks repeatedly has acknowledged his indebtedness to the work of the anthropologist Clifford Geertz, who coined the term, "thick description."

15. Wayne A. Meeks, *The First Urban Christians: The Social World of the Apostle Paul* (New Haven: Yale University Press, 1983).

16. Wayne A. Meeks, *The Moral World of the First Christians* (Library of Early Christianity) (Philadelphia: Westminster, 1986).

17. Meeks, *The Origins of Christian Morality,* 4.

18. An English translation of Wrede's famous essay is available in R. Morgan, ed., *The Nature of New Testament Theology: The Contribution of William Wrede and Adolf Schlatter* (Studies in Biblical Theology, Second Series, 35) (London: SCM, 1973).

19. Meeks, *Origins,* 211.

20. Ibid., 213–219.

21. Hays, *Moral Vision,* 215–225.

22. Eduard Lohse, *Theological Ethics of the New Testament,* trans. M. Eugene Boring (Minneapolis: Augsburg, 1991).

23. Elisabeth Schüssler Fiorenza, "The Will to Choose or to Reject: Continuing Our Critical Work," in Letty M. Russell, ed., *Feminist Interpretation of the Bible* (Philadelphia: Westminster Press, 1985), 130.

24. Elisabeth Schüssler Fiorenza, *Bread Not Stone: The Challenge of Feminist Biblical Interpretation* (Boston: Beacon Press, 1984), 145.

25. Ibid., 88.

26. E. Schüssler Fiorenza, *In Memory of Her: A Feminist Theological Reconstruction of Christian Origins* (New York: Crossroad, 1983), 35.

27. Willi Marxsen, *New Testament Foundations for Christian Ethics,* trans. O.C. Dean, Jr. (Minneapolis: Fortress Press, 1993).

28. Schüssler Fiorenza, *In Memory of Her,* 32.

29. Stanley Hauerwas, *A Community of Character: Toward a Constructive Christian Social Ethic* (Notre Dame, Ind.: University of Notre Dame Press, 1981), 36. The quotation is taken from Athanasius, *The Incarnation of the Word of God.* The importance of this passage for Hauerwas is suggested by the fact that he cites it again in full in *Unleashing the Scripture: Freeing the Bible from Captivity to America* (Nashville: Abingdon, 1993), 37–38.

30. Hauerwas, *Community of Character,* 1 (emphasis mine).

31. Hauerwas, *Unleashing the Scripture,* 15.

32. Ibid., 15.

33. Fowl, Stephen E. and L. Gregory Jones, *Reading in Communion: Scripture and Ethics in the Christian Life* (Grand Rapids: Eerdmans, 1991).

34. Daniel Patte, *Ethics of Biblical Interpretation: A Reevaluation* (Louisville: Westminster John Knox, 1995).

35. Hauerwas, *Unleashing the Scripture,* 36.

RETELLING THE STORY
THE RULE OF FAITH AND
THE TASK OF NEW TESTAMENT ETHICS

In this lecture, I aim to summarize concisely the approach to New Testament ethics that I have set forth in my book, *The Moral Vision of the New Testament*. I know that some of you have already read it; I must beg your indulgence for repeating some material that will already be familiar to you. This material constitutes an essential framework for the fourth lecture, in which I tackle the issue of the relationship between men and women in the church. Therefore, since I do not presume that all of you will have read the book, I must take the time to explain the approach that I am taking. Even for those of you who have already read the book, I hope that there will be some value in this summary of my proposed method for employing the New Testament in the work of moral discernment—particularly because I hope, along the way, to amplify and clarify certain points about the relation of my method to the confessional traditions of historic Christianity.

The Four-Fold Task of New Testament Ethics

I would suggest that New Testament ethics—understood as a normative theological discipline—entails four overlapping critical operations: the *descriptive,* the *synthetic,* the *hermeneutical,* and the *pragmatic* tasks. For present purposes, I will offer brief capsule definitions of each of these tasks.

The *descriptive* task is to read the New Testament texts as carefully as possible, attending to the distinctive message of each of the individual witnesses in the New Testament canon. This means attending not only to explicit moral teachings but also to the moral world manifest in the stories, symbols, social structures, and practices that shape the community's *ethos.* A text such as the Gospel of John, for example, may have relatively little explicit ethical teaching, but its story of a "man from heaven" who comes to reveal God's truth to an unbelieving world is fraught with ethical implications for the community that accepts the message and finds itself rejected by the world.

The *synthetic* task is to place the individual witnesses side by side and to ask whether they are coherent. Is it possible to describe a unity of ethical perspective within the diversity of the canon? This is the phase of the operation that Wayne Meeks deems impossible; he takes the canon's ideological diversity to be irreducible.[1] I would contend, on the contrary, that the task of discerning some coherence in the canon is both necessary and possible. The difficult problem, however, is to know what methods might allow us to give an appropriate account of this canonical coherence. This problem is not always clearly confronted in the literature on New Testament ethics. What—if anything—makes these diverse writings hang together as a guide to the moral life?

However, even if we should succeed in giving some satisfactory synthetic account of the New Testament's ethical content, we will still find ourselves at the brink of a daunting abyss: the temporal and cultural distance between ourselves and the text. How can we bridge this chasm? This is the *hermeneutical* task. How do we appropriate the New Testament's message as a word addressed to us? These texts were not written in the first instance for North Americans at the end of the twentieth century. When we read Paul's letters to his churches, we are reading the mail of people who have been dead for nineteen hundred years; when we read the Gospels, we are reading stories told for the benefit of ancient communities whose customs and problems differed vastly from ours. Only historical ignorance or cultural chauvinism could lead us to suppose that no hermeneutical "translation" is necessary for us to understand these texts. The more we understand, the more we will find ourselves wondering how we can take our moral bearings from a world so different from ours. If the New Testament's teachings are so integrally imbedded in the social and symbolic world of first-century communities, can they speak at all to us or for us?

The final task of New Testament ethics is the *pragmatic* task: embodying Scripture's imperatives in the life of the Christian community. Without this living embodiment of the word, none of the above deliberation matters. The test that finally proves the value of our theological labors is the "fruits test:" "A good tree cannot bear bad fruit, nor can a bad tree bear good fruit. . . .Thus you will know them by their fruits" (Matthew 7:18,20). The value of our exegesis and hermeneutics will be tested by their capacity to produce persons and communities whose character is commensurate with Jesus Christ and thereby pleasing to God.

Some readers will find this four-fold division of the task to be artificial. Does my design encourage an illusion that exegesis is an objective science and that hermeneutical concerns can be deferred until a late stage in the interpretive process? To be sure, the four tasks described here always overlap in practice. The work of description and synthesis can never be wholly divorced from the interpreter's hermeneutical concerns, and our own experience of the pragmatic enactment of Scripture will condition our reading from start to finish. No one should suppose, then, that the four tasks are simple sequential steps; when Scripture is actually employed in the church, the interpreter integrates the four tasks. Nonetheless, it is useful to break the tasks of interpretation down for analytic purposes. This heuristic division of the tasks gives us a way of systematically reviewing our integrative judgments and uses of the New Testament.

The work of *descriptive* exegesis requires patient attention to the close reading of texts; this is hardly an exercise that can be undertaken in a programmatic lecture of this sort. (In the fourth lecture on the issue of the New Testament's teaching concerning the relation of men and women in the church, I will offer a brief illustration of how this descriptive work might be done.) For now, I will reluctantly bracket out the first of the four tasks I have identified and offer some proposals about the rest of the process: the *synthetic, hermeneutical,* and *pragmatic* dimensions of New Testament ethics. First, I want to offer you a proposal about how to discern the unity of the New Testament's ethical witness; then, I want to address one aspect of the hermeneutical task by arguing that the use of Scripture in normative ethics is necessarily an exercise of the metaphorical imagination; finally, with regard to the pragmatic task, I will offer a few remarks about the formation of community as the *telos* of New Testament ethics.

Three Focal Images: Community, Cross, New Creation

The unity that we discover in the New Testament is not the unity of a dogmatic system. Rather, the unity that we find is the looser unity of a collection of documents that, in various ways, retell and comment upon a single fundamental story. That story may be summarized roughly as follows:

> The God of Israel, the creator of all that exists, has acted (astoundingly) to rescue a lost and broken world through the death and resurrection of Jesus; the full scope of that rescue is not yet apparent, but God has created a community of witnesses to this good news, the church. While awaiting the grand conclusion of the story, the church, empowered by the Holy Spirit, is called to reenact the loving obedience of Jesus Christ and thus to serve as a sign of God's redemptive purposes for the world.

I acknowledge that it certainly is controversial for me to assert that Scripture tells a "single focused story." Many interpreters of the Bible are far more impressed by its diversity or disunity than by the presence of a unifying narrative thread. [For example, Käsemann's famous address to the World Council of Churches at which he argued polemically that the New Testament canon is the basis of the disunity of the church, not of its unity.] What is the basis, then, for my assertion of a narrative unity?

For the conference at Duke (to which I referred in the first lecture), George Lindbeck wrote a perceptive response to my then-unpublished manuscript of *The Moral Vision of the New Testament*, in which he suggested that my approach is far more indebted than I had acknowledged to "the mainstream Christian tradition of canonical reading which goes back to Irenaeus." Furthermore, he observed, its "theological framework . . . is fully consistent with the christological, trinitarian, and anti-Marcionite decisions of the church." It seems to me that Lindbeck's point is well taken. My account of a narrative unity in the New Testament canon is dependent upon a mode of reading, a set of implicit foreunderstandings that governed the formation of the New Testament canon to begin with and which have been passed along in the church through the centuries since then. I am able to read these texts as telling a "single fundamental story" in part because I have been trained by the church's creeds, liturgy, and hymns to discern that story there. And of course, in this respect I am hardly distinctive: I share this legacy with Christians throughout the ages.

One way of understanding the brief plot synopsis I have just given is to see it as a contemporary reformulation of "the Rule of Faith." This is a term coined by Irenaeus at the end of the second century to refer to the content of the church's proclamation, "that which has always been believed everywhere by everyone" in the church catholic. This "Rule" was never given any one definitive verbal formulation; it could be expressed—or *performed*—in various ways, but it always stood as a shorthand narrative summary of the one gospel proclaimed through the apostolic writings and believed in the church. Thus, when I offer my own summary, I am doing nothing more adventurous than chiming in to the chorus of historic orthodox Christian confession through the ages and insisting that this confession provides the narrative grounding for a unified reading of Scripture.

One way of putting this point would be to say that—truth to be told—my model 6 has to be subsumed within Hauerwas's model 5, or at least linked with it. I am making a suggestion about how we as the church ought to articulate the unity that we have been taught to perceive intuitively in the biblical story. For those who are disposed to be skeptical, there is no way to "prove" the truth of this perception. All we can do is retell the story, call people to read the texts, and trust that our account will commend itself as readers open themselves to hear the Word.

But this still does not address the problem of the actual diversity of expressions or "tellings" of the story within the New Testament itself. A different "spin" is put on the story by each New Testament writer; for example, we find widely different evaluations of the degree of continuity between Israel and the church. Consequently, it would be impossible—or, at best, infelicitous—to put these different accounts into the blender so as to produce a single harmonized telling of the story, a late-twentieth-century Diatessaron.

What we can do, however—and this is central to my present constructive proposal—is to identify certain key *images* that all the different canonical tellings share. Such images encapsulate the crucial elements of the narrative and serve to focus our attention on the common ground shared by the various witnesses. Thus they serve as *lenses* to focus our reading of the New Testament: when we reread the canonical documents through these images, our blurry multiple impressions of the texts come more sharply into focus.

Further, no single image can adequately encapsulate the complex unity of the New Testament texts. Because these texts retell and interpret a narrative, their message reflects the complexity and temporal movement of emplotted experience; consequently, we need a cluster—or a sequence—of images to represent the underlying story and bring it into focus. I suggest three focal images as guidelines for synthetic reflection about the New Testament canon: *community*, *cross*, and *new creation*.

Community: *The church is a counter-cultural community of discipleship, and this community is the primary addressee of God's imperatives.* The biblical story focuses on God's design for forming a covenant people. Thus, the primary sphere of moral concern is not the character of the individual but the corporate obedience of the church. Paul's formulation in Romans 12:1–2 encapsulates the vision: "Present your bodies [*sōmata*, plural] as *a* living sacrifice [*thysian*, singular], holy and well-pleasing to God. And do not be conformed to this age, but be transformed by the renewing of your mind. . . ." The community, in its corporate life, is called to embody an alternative order that stands as a sign of God's redemptive purposes in the world. (This is, of course, a theme historically emphasized by the Anabaptist tradition.) Many New Testament texts express different facets of this image: the church is the body of Christ, a temple built of living stones, a city set on a hill, Israel in the wilderness. The coherence of the New Testament's ethical mandate will come into focus only when we understand that mandate in *ecclesial* terms, when we seek God's will not by asking first, "What should I do," but "What should we do?"

Cross: *Jesus' death on a cross is the paradigm for faithfulness to God in this world.* The community expresses and experiences the presence of the kingdom of God by participating in "the *koinōnia* of his sufferings" (Philippians 3:10). Jesus' death is consistently interpreted in the New Testament as an act of self-giving love, and the community is consistently called to take up the cross and follow in the way that his death defines. The death of Jesus carries with it the promise of the resurrection, but the power of the resurrection is in God's hands, not ours. Therefore, our actions are to be judged not by their calculable efficacy in producing desirable results but by their correspondence to Jesus' example. Consequently, the role of the community appears paradoxical: "While we live, we are always being given up to death for Jesus' sake, so that the life of Jesus may be manifested in our mortal flesh" (2 Corinthians 4:11). That is the vocation and job description of the church. Common sense protests this account of Christian faithfulness, just as Peter did when he was scandalized by Jesus' talk of cross-bearing (Mark 8:31–38), but the New Testament texts witness univocally to the *imitatio Christi* as the way of obedience.

In view of the historic abuse of the theme of the cross in patriarchal cultures, and in view of the recent reaction against this theme by some feminist theologians, an additional word of clarification is necessary in order to avert misunderstanding. The image of the cross should not be used by those who hold power in order to insure the acquiescent suffering of the powerless. Instead, the New Testament insists that the community as a whole is called to follow in the way of Jesus' suffering. The New Testament writers consistently employ the pattern of the cross precisely to call those who possess power and privilege to *surrender* it for the sake of the weak. In the New Testament's one clear application of this pattern to the patriarchal marriage relationship, it is husbands (not wives) who are called to emulate Christ's example of giving themselves up in obedience for the sake of the other (Ephesians 5:25). To read such a text—which calls for husbands to love and tenderly care for their wives—as though it somehow warranted a husband's domination or physical abuse of his wife can only be regarded as bizarre and blasphemous misreading. It is precisely the focal image of the cross that ensures that the followers of Jesus will read the New Testament as a call to renounce violence.

New Creation: *The church embodies the power of the resurrection in the midst of a not-yet-redeemed world.* Paul's image of "new creation" stands here as a shorthand signifier for the dialectical eschatology that runs throughout the New Testament.[2] In the present time, the new creation already appears, but only proleptically; consequently, we hang in suspense between Jesus' resurrection and parousia. "The whole creation has been groaning in travail together until now; and not only the creation, but we ourselves, who have the first fruits of the spirit, groan inwardly as we wait for adoption, the redemption of our bodies" (Romans 8:22–23). The eschatological framework of life in Christ imparts to Christian existence its strange temporal sensibility, its odd capacity for simultaneous joy amidst suffering and impatience with things as they are. We can never say—like the guys in a popular TV beer commercial—"It doesn't get any better than this," because we know it will; we are, like T. S. Eliot's Magi, "no longer at ease here, in the old dispensation." The church is, in Paul's remarkable phrase, the community of those "upon whom the ends of the ages have met" (1 Corinthians 10:11).[3] In Christ, we know that the powers of the old age are doomed, and the new creation is already appearing. Yet, at the same time, all attempts to assert the unqualified presence of the kingdom of God stand under judgment of the eschatological reservation: not before the time, not yet. Thus the New Testament's eschatology creates a critical framework that pronounces judgment upon our complacency as well as upon our presumptuous despair. As often as we eat the bread and drink the cup, we proclaim the Lord's *death . . . until he comes.* Within that anomalous hope-filled interval, all the New Testament writers work out their understandings of God's will for the community.

The function of these three synthetic images must be kept clearly in mind. They should not be treated as principles that can be applied independently to the analysis of ethical issues without reference to the texts from which they are derived; rather, they are *lenses* that bring our reading of the canonical texts into sharper focus, as we seek to discern what is central or fundamental in the ethical witness of the New Testament as a whole.

It should be stressed again that this proposal of three focal images offers what Lindbeck calls a "performance interpretation" of the unity of the New Testament canon. Every synthetic account of the unity of the New Testament's moral vision will necessarily be an imaginative construct of the interpreter—or perhaps better, of the interpretive community. (This, by the way, is a decisive refutation of the protest of one reviewer who accused me of trying to produce a book that will offer an airtight method for settling ethical disputes.) Every unifying construal is a "performance," analogous to a director's reading of a Shakespeare play—a reading that seeks to discern and articulate the shape and meaning of the whole. The value of the performance must be tested by others in the community who will bear witness concerning whether or not this performance satisfyingly illuminates the wholeness of the canon.

Moral Judgment as Metaphor-Making

I turn now to some remarks about the hermeneutical task of New Testament ethics. Under this heading, we may identify provisionally issues of two different types: (a) how to balance or correlate the authority of Scripture with the authority of other sources of moral guidance (often categorized as tradition, reason, and experience); and (b) the *mode* in which Scripture functions in shaping moral judgments. The former issue lies beyond the scope of my present concerns, but I want to give some attention to the latter.

James Gustafson's article of twenty-five years ago, "The Place of Scripture in Christian Ethics," delineated a typology of ways of using Scripture in the formation of normative judgment: we may appeal to Scripture as a source of moral law, or of moral ideals, or of historical analogies to our present circumstances, or—somewhat vaguely—of a "great variety" of "moral values, moral norms and principles" which may be eclectically appropriated by the Christian theologian.[4] I would like to reformulate Gustafson's categories slightly and speak of Scripture as a source of: (a) rules; (b) principles; (c) paradigms for action; or (d) a symbolic world that governs our understanding of God and of the human situation. If, as I suggested above, the form in which the New Testament witnesses present themselves to us is predominantly *narrative,* it will follow that the latter two ways of using Scripture (paradigmatic and world-shaping) will be more characteristic and more important than the former two (rules and principles). The New Testament canon addresses ethical issues not primarily by giving laws or by reasoning abstractly from philosophical principles but rather by telling stories into which we find ourselves caught up.

If that is right, when we seek to practice New Testament

ethics we will find ourselves necessarily formulating metaphorical correspondences between the stories told in the texts and the story lived out by our community in a very different historical setting. Hermeneutics requires *an integrative act of the imagination.* This is always so, even for those who would like to deny it: with fear and trembling we must work out a life of faithfulness to God through responsive and creative reappropriation of the New Testament in a world far removed from the world of the original writers and readers. *Thus, whenever we appeal to the authority of the New Testament, we are necessarily engaged in metaphor-making, placing our community's life imaginatively within the world articulated by the texts.* An exercise of aesthetic judgment is unavoidable if the two worlds are to be brought into conjunction.

Metaphors are incongruous conjunctions of two images that turn out, upon reflection, to be like one another in ways not ordinarily recognized. They shock us into thought by positing unexpected analogies. Thus, metaphors reshape perception. For example, when the Gospel of John presents Jesus as saying "I am the living bread that came down from heaven" (John 6:51a), the message jolts his hearers, who are looking for him to play the role of Moses by providing them with miraculous bread to eat (6:30–31). Jesus' striking response refuses the identification with Moses and posits instead a metaphorical conjunction between himself and the manna that fed the Israelites in the wilderness. The metaphor quickly takes a gruesome turn when Jesus goes on to say that "the bread that I will give for the life of the world is my flesh" and to affirm that "those who eat my flesh and drink my blood have eternal life" (6:51b,54a). At one level, the metaphorical shock induces the reader to confront the scandal of John's claim that "the word became flesh;" at the same time, the metaphor leads the reader to make the imaginative connection between the exodus story and the church's eucharist, with the flesh of Jesus as the startling common term. The hearer of such a metaphor is confronted by two options. We can take offense at this jarring conjunction of images, as did those disciples who went away murmuring, "This teaching is difficult; who can accept it?" (John 6:61). Or, alternatively, we can "understand" the metaphor. To "understand" it, however, is to stand under its authority, to allow one's life and perception of reality to be changed, so that we confess with Peter, "Lord, to whom (else) can we go? You have the words of eternal life" (6:68).

The metaphorical process can occur not only at the level of the individual image or sentence, but also at the higher level of the story, as we see in the parables of the synoptic gospels. Luke's parable of the dishonest manager (Luke 16:1–9), for instance, offers an unsettling narrative of a shrewd operator who, on the verge of being fired by his master, ingratiates himself to the master's debtors by settling accounts at a dramatic discount. In the parable's surprise punch line, the master, rather than being still more furious at the manager, commends him for his savvy dealings! We readers, expecting that the parable will end with a tidy moral condemnation of the dishonest manager, are caught off guard and forced to reconsider our understanding of the moral order of things. Why does the master not condemn the servant? Perhaps it is because he recognized that the moment of judgment was at hand and acted decisively, just as the hearers of Jesus' message of the kingdom of God are called to respond decisively rather than continuing with business as usual. Our discomfort with this conclusion to the tale forces us to recognize our affinity with the priggish older brother in the parable of the prodigal son (Luke 15:11–32), which immediately precedes the parable of the dishonest manager in Luke's story. Like the older brother, we stand offended outside the celebration if we continue to insist that people ought to get what is coming to them. To "understand" these parables is to be changed by them, to have our vision of the world reshaped by them. To "understand" them is to enter the process of reflecting about how our lives ought to change in response to the gospel.

A similar reorientation of our perceptions occurs—on an even larger scale—when we read and come to "understand" the

Gospels that tell the story of a crucified Messiah. This story is "a stumbling block to Jews and foolishness to Gentiles, but to those who are the called, both Jews and Greeks, Christ the power of God and the wisdom of God" (1 Corinthians 1:23–24). The fundamental task of New Testament ethics is to call us again and again to see our lives anew by reading them in metaphorical juxtaposition with this story. This metaphorical reading process engenders a "conversion of the imagination." The world we know—or thought we knew—is reconfigured when we "read" it in counterpoint with the New Testament. The hermeneutical task is to relocate our contemporary experience on the map of the New Testament's story of Jesus. By telling a story that overturns our conventional ways of seeing the world, the New Testament provides the images and categories in light of which the life of our community is reinterpreted.[5] Thus, the temporal gap between first-century Christians and Christians at the end of the twentieth century can be bridged only by a spark of imagination.

The great difficulty, of course, lies in knowing how to judge the validity of proposed metaphorical appropriations of the New Testament. There are no foolproof procedures. Our metaphorical readings must be tested prayerfully within the community of faith by others who seek God's will along with us through close reading of the text. The community that seeks to be shaped by Scripture must in the end claim responsibility for adjudicating between good and bad readings by asking whether any given interpretation is consonant with the fundamental plot of the biblical story as identified by the focal images of community, cross, and new creation.

The Church as Embodied Metaphor

Finally, the task of discerning metaphorical relations between the New Testament and the present time shades imperceptibly into the *pragmatic* task of shaping our communities into living embodiments of the meaning of the New Testament texts. Such a vision for the church may sound like visionary fantasy, far removed from a realistic empirical assessment. But one of the

New Testament's most important lessons for Christian ethics is that we should dream big and audaciously discern the presence of the kingdom even where the world does not yet see much evidence of it.

Writing to his unruly and immature little congregation in Corinth, Paul coins a startling metaphor: "You are a letter of Christ, . . . written not with ink but with the Spirit of the living God, not on tablets of stone but on the tablets of fleshy hearts" (2 Corinthians 3:3).[6] Despite their squabbles and peccadillos, he does not say to them, "Shape up; don't you know you're supposed to be a letter from Christ?" Instead, with metaphorical audacity, he says, "You *are* a letter from Christ . . . to be known and read by all." The existence of this struggling community is a communication of the gospel to the world.

This remarkable claim opens a crucial insight into the hermeneutical relation between text and community, between the New Testament and the church. If moral judgment entails—as I argued above—the making of metaphors through which the New Testament reconfigures our understanding of our communal identity, the converse is also true: the transformed community reflects the glory of God and thus illuminates the meaning of the text. According to Paul, apart from Christ a veil lies over the minds of the hearers when Scripture is read.

> But when one turns to the Lord, the veil is removed. . . . And all of us, with unveiled faces, seeing the glory of the Lord as though reflected in a mirror, are being transformed into the same image from one degree of glory to another (2 Corinthians 3:16,18).

Thus, the church itself, being transformed into the image of Christ, becomes a living metaphor for the power of God to which the text also bears witness.[7] The text shapes the community, and the community embodies the meaning of the text. Thus, there is a hermeneutical feedback loop that generates fresh readings of the New Testament as the community grows in maturity and as it confronts changing situations.

These observations lead us to state a final dimension of the hermeneutical task: *right reading of the New Testament occurs only where the word is embodied.* We learn what the text means only if we submit ourselves to its power in such a way that we are changed by it. That is why George Steiner, in his important book *Real Presences*, wants to define hermeneutics as "the enactment of answerable understanding, of active apprehension."[8] The interpretative enterprise is not completed by the work of analysis and commentary; to interpret a text rightly is to put it to work, to perform it in a way that is self-involving so that our interpretations become acts of "commitment at risk."[9] As Nicholas Lash argues in his essay "Performing the Scriptures," "the fundamental form of the *Christian* interpretation of scripture is the life, activity, and organization of the believing community."[10]

One consequence of this hermeneutical guideline is that interpretation of the New Testament cannot be performed by isolated individuals; the embodiment of the word happens in the body of Christ, the church. Hermeneutics is necessarily a communal activity. "The performance of scripture," contends Lash, "*is* the life of the church. It is no more possible for an isolated individual to perform *these* texts than it is for him to perform a Beethoven quartet or a Shakespeare tragedy."[11]

Of course it is paradoxical to assert that we can understand Scripture only after we see it enacted. Is it not necessary to have some understanding before action is possible? Two approaches to grasping this paradox may be suggested.

First, we are not starting from nowhere, reading the New Testament as though it had just been found sealed in a cave; we are the heirs of a community that has been reading and performing these texts for nineteen hundred years already. We can point to prior performances that illuminate the meaning of the text. As Stanley Hauerwas says, "The lives of the saints are the hermeneutical key to Scripture."

Secondly, as anyone who has ever participated in a dramatic production or a group musical performance or even a team sport can attest, something happens in the act of performance that transcends the experience of private rehearsal. The curtain goes up, the audience reacts, the interaction with other performers takes on an unforeseeable chemistry, and by the end of the play we have learned something we had not known before. In the best case, the serious performance of the great text, we learn something not only about the text but about ourselves as well.[12]

The New Testament itself repeatedly insists on the necessity of embodiment of the word. The sequence of the verbs in Romans 12:1–2 is significant: "*Present* your bodies as a living sacrifice. [Hear the metaphor!] . . . Be transformed . . . that you may prove what is the will of God, what is good and acceptable and perfect." Knowledge of the will of God *follows* the community's submission and transformation. Why? Because until we see the text lived, we cannot begin to conceive what it means. Until we see God's power at work among us we do not know what we are reading. Thus, the most crucial hermeneutical task is the formation of communities that retell the story by seeking to live under the word.

Notes

1. Wayne A. Meeks, "Understanding Early Christian Ethics," *Journal of Biblical Literature* 105 (1986): 3–11.

2. The Gospel of John is the one New Testament text that may not fit easily into this synthetic account. John's emphasis on the realized element of eschatology is so strong that it threatens to dissolve the tension of unrealized promise found elsewhere in the New Testament. However, this Gospel continues to look forward to a resurrection "at the last day," which cannot be identified with the fulfillment of coming to know Jesus in the present life. Also, when the Gospel is read in canonical context along with 1 John, the future eschatological emphasis is more clearly preserved: see, for example, 1 John 2:25, 3:2, 4:17.

3. Most English translations of this passage obscure Paul's conviction that the community stands at the point of collision or overlapping of two ages. See J. Louis Martyn, "Epistemology at the Turn of the Ages," in *Theological Issues in the Letters of Paul* (Nashville: Abingdon, 1997), 89–110.

4. J.M. Gustafson, "The Place of Scripture in Christian Ethics," *Interpretation* 24 (1970): 439–445.

5. Of course, the metaphorical juxtaposition allows the transfer of meaning both ways. The community also reinterprets the text in light of the church's experience.

6. For discussion of the passage and explanation of this translation, see Richard B. Hays, *Echoes of Scripture in the Letters of Paul* (New Haven: Yale University Press, 1989), 125–131.

7. For more extensive discussion, see Hays, *Echoes of Scripture,* 131–149.

8. George Steiner, *Real Presences* (Chicago: University of Chicago Press, 1989), 7.

9. Ibid., 8.

10. Nicholas Lash, *Theology on the Way to Emmaus* (London: SCM Press, 1986), 42. Cf., Steiner, *Real Presences,* 8: "The true hermeneutic of drama is staging."

11. Lash, *Theology on the Way to Emmaus,* 43.

12. Ibid., 41.

THE SIGNIFICANCE OF THE HISTORICAL JESUS FOR CHRISTIAN ETHICS

This lecture will deal with the problem of the significance of the historical Jesus for Christian ethics. Should a treatment of New Testament ethics begin with a historical reconstruction of the teaching of Jesus? As I noted in the last lecture, Wolfgang Schrage, who conceives of New Testament ethics as a historical project, answers this question affirmatively. Consequently, he makes the methodological decision to open his book with a very long chapter, more than 100 pages in length, on the ethics proclaimed by the Jesus of history. This has been a typical way for New Testament scholars, writing books on New Testament ethics, to organize their work. On the other hand, in my book, *The Moral Vision of the New Testament,* I argue that New Testament ethics should be concerned primarily with the content of the canonical portraits of the life and teachings of Jesus, rather than with a historian's reconstruction of the events behind these portrayals. Therefore, I place the discussion of the role of the historical Jesus in a brief excursus of about ten pages which follows individual chapters the four canonical Gospels, each one considered in its own right as a primary voice in the New Testament chorus.

This procedure has attracted some controversy from various sides. Some reviewers have questioned my decision to give such a minor place to the historical Jesus in a presentation of New Testament ethics; on the other hand, at least one reviewer, Luke Timothy Johnson, has criticized my book for paying any attention to the question at all. He describes my short chapter on Jesus as "an unfortunately wrong turn." He continues as follows: "Not only does Hays inadvertently play directly into the hands of those who wish to hold the Christian tradition hostage to the ever-shifting conclusions of historical inquiry, but he diminishes the critical role played by convictions concerning Jesus' death and resurrection for shaping the image of Jesus that stands at the heart of Hays' single fundamental story."[1] Another way to put Johnson's point would be as follows: The image of Jesus that matters for New Testament ethics is the image portrayed by the kerygma, the proclaimed Gospel of the Church. Therefore, what historians say about Jesus simply does not matter. And Johnson thinks that for me even to treat it in an excursus in the book is to give hostages to fortune.

In light of these responses, I want to reopen the question. What can we really know about the Jesus of history? And what role should our account of Jesus as a historical figure play in New Testament ethics?

When confronted by this difficult question, I always recall an apocryphal story about Paul Tillich. It seems that back in the 1950s, a team of Roman Catholic archaeologists conducting a dig in Jerusalem discovered the tomb of Jesus and found, to their horror, his bones still in the tomb. They dutifully called the Pope and informed him of this disturbing discovery. The Pope decided that before making any sort of public statement, he should convene a secret ecumenical council to ponder the church's response to this crisis. And so he asked his advisors, "Who is the greatest Protestant theologian?" He was told it was Paul Tillich. (Of course, he was misinformed about that: it was Karl Barth. But never mind.) So the Pope placed a long-distance phone call to Tillich at Union Theological Seminary in New York and carefully explained the troubling news that the archaeologists had found the bones of Jesus still in the tomb. There was a long silence at the other end of the line. Finally, Tillich responded, "So then, he really did live!"

We chuckle at this story because it plays upon a strange fact of our recent theological history: much twentieth-century theology has assumed that the Jesus of history is unknowable. Thus, Tillich tried to formulate a christology that was detached from the Jesus of history. And he was by no means alone in this. He was, of course, influenced by Rudolf Bultmann, and much New Testament scholarship in the middle of this century under Bultmann's influence was engaged in a similar project. In his theology of the New Testament, Bultmann famously argued that the preaching of Jesus does not belong to the theology of the New Testament, properly speaking, but rather to the presuppositions of a theology of the New Testament. Recently, however, in about the last 15 to 20 years, we've seen a renewed effort to give a purely historical account of Jesus, an account free from the control of Christian doctrine and tradition. I say a renewed effort, because in many respects this recent quest is nothing other than the revival of nineteenth-century liberalism's project of portraying Jesus as a model of enlightened reason, separated decisively from anything too Jewish and particularly separated from any taint of apocalyptic eschatology.

The most notorious purveyors of this new fictional, non-Jewish Jesus have been, of course, the members of the Jesus Seminar, led by Robert Funk, John Dominic Crossan, and Burton Mack. Their influence has spread widely. Some of you may have seen, for instance, an exchange of letters in *The Christian Century,* in which a reader protested against an article I had published there. The reader, an ordained Episcopal priest, asserted that "the Gospels do not reveal Jesus. Instead they reveal what various first century communities wanted themselves and others to believe about Jesus."[2] There have been several devastating critiques of the Jesus Seminar offered by serious New Testament scholars, particularly by Luke Timothy Johnson and N.T. Wright. Therefore, I am not going to waste your time by offering an extended rebuttal to the work of the Jesus Seminar. Suffice it to say that I think their work is tendentious fantasy. It is deeply flawed in its methods, and no one should regard its findings as serious critical history.

More pertinent to the question I want to raise today are the issues posed by Johnson in his book, *The Real Jesus: The Misguided Quest for the Historical Jesus and the Truth of the*

Traditional Gospels. (Johnson wins the award, I think, for the most clearly polemical book title of recent years.) After exposing the absurdity of the claims of the Jesus Seminar, Johnson goes on to argue that Christian faith has never been based on the historical Jesus. Rather, he writes, "Christian faith then and now is based on religious claims concerning the present power of Jesus."[3] As Johnson explains it, history is a very limited mode of knowing that cannot deal at all with the truths that are the most important and most real. Especially the resurrection of Jesus, Johnson insists, simply is not an event that is accessible to historical inquiry. So the "real Jesus" of Johnson's title is the living Lord encountered in the church's present experience. We know this living Lord not through historical inquiry, but through encountering his transforming power in our lives. Indeed, Johnson seems virtually to equate the meaning of resurrection with this experience of transforming power now in the church. As a Roman Catholic, he tends to assume that this encounter occurs through the mediation of tradition and sacrament. In other words, Johnson's book responds to the question, "What can we really know about Jesus?" by carefully reframing the meaning of the verb "to know." What we know most certainly is not to be found, Johnson argues, in the realm of fact and history, but rather in the realm of religious experience.

In my judgment, this is a theologically perilous move. By placing history and truth in separate compartments, Johnson reinforces the post-Kantian split between faith and history in a way that I find deeply problematical. I want to argue instead, that faith and history stand necessarily in a dialogical relationship with one another. Precisely because of the character of the New Testament witnesses themselves, faith cannot cut itself loose from history in the way that Johnson recommends. I propose then to do two things: First, I offer a brief response to Johnson by indicating why we should care about the historical Jesus, and why our investigation of this problem might be significant for New Testament ethics, which, after all, is the overall concern of these lectures. Second, I want to engage the recent work of N.T.

Wright, particularly his major new book, *Jesus and the Victory of God*,[4] and explore how Wright's particular proposals about the Jesus of history might be significant for New Testament ethics. This juxtaposition of Johnson and Wright nicely illustrates the issues that I want to discuss.

First, then, why should we care about the historical Jesus? As I've indicated, Luke Johnson has posed a strong challenge to the project of reconstructing the historical Jesus by arguing that the things that really matter are not accessible to historical investigation and that the real Jesus is known to the church in its living experience, not through historical reconstruction. In light of this challenge, why should we, as historians and as Christians, undertake the effort to explore what we can know historically about the figure of Jesus? As we try to sort this out, it is important to make a distinction between the Jesus of history, that is, the flesh and blood human being Jesus of Nazareth who lived in first-century Palestine, and the historian's reconstruction of that figure. The phrase "historical Jesus" is ambiguous because it can mean either of those two things, and they are not precisely identical. The historian's reconstruction is always, at best, an account, a tentative approximation of the historical figure himself. But there is no knowledge of that historical figure except through some such reconstruction. Indeed, our canonical Gospels, I would argue, are in fact the earliest attempt to render such accounts of that historical figure even though they are not "histories" in the modern sense of that word.

Our reasons for attending to this project of interpreting Jesus historically are at least three: first, we're compelled to do it by the character of the New Testament witnesses themselves; second, we're compelled to it by the question of truth; and third, we're compelled to it as a theological matter by the internal logic of Christian doctrine.

The character of the New Testament witnesses themselves. It is a very significant fact that we have four Gospels in our New Testament canon, not just one. The church was emphatic early on in rejecting the move of Marcion to limit the Gospel canon by cutting it down to a single Gospel, and it was equally emphatic in rejecting Tatian's Diatessaron, which was an effort to produce a single Gospel harmony that conflated all four together. There was an insistence on retaining the four-fold Gospel canon, four distinct and different portraits. How are we to account for this?

When I teach Introduction to the New Testament for students in seminary, I do not begin with the historical Jesus. This is the way New Testament courses have traditionally been taught: you start with the historical Jesus; then you speculate about the traditions concerning him in the early oral tradition in the community; finally you examine how the Gospel writers as redactors pulled those traditions together into the compositions that now exist. Instead of doing that, I begin by looking in sequential order at the four canonical portraits, just the four different pictures that are painted there of Jesus. By the time we get to the end of looking at those four portraits, most of my students are practically climbing the walls wanting to ask the historical question: "Yes, but what really happened? What's behind this?" Why? Because they see that these stories are told differently. For example, the Gospel of John places Jesus' action of driving the money-changers out of the temple at the beginning of the narrative instead of at the end as in the Synoptics. Why is that? Which way is right? Which way did it happen? There are various ways to deal with this problem, but one of the unavoidable ways is to try to understand what history lies behind the accounts and how and why they developed in the way they did.

A second aspect of the character of the New Testament witnesses themselves is that these Gospel texts are referential narratives. That is, they tell stories about events that happened in the past—the recent past for the original authors and readers—and they ask readers to accept these accounts as true. Consider the prologue of Luke's Gospel (Luke 1:1–4). He says, "I've been investigating these things for some time, and I want to set down an orderly account in order that you might be given confidence of the truth of the things you have been taught." The question about the Jesus of history arises, then, not merely because of some unbelieving perversity, but because of the form in which the Gospels themselves have chosen to bear witness. Unlike the church's historic creeds, the Gospels do not skip from Jesus' virgin birth to his crucifixion under Pontius Pilate with nothing in between. You know how the creed goes: "Born of the Virgin Mary, suffered under Pontius Pilate." And apparently nothing happened in between those events! But the Gospels are not like that. His teachings and healings, his eating with sinners, and his other doings are narrated as crucial disclosures of his identity. Surely there is something at stake in the question of whether these stories correspond to real events in space-time history.

Johnson's desire to place history and faith in separate hermetically sealed spheres would have been unintelligible to the Gospel writers and even to Paul, who believed that if you were inclined to doubt the resurrection, you could go ask those 500 brethren, most of whom were still alive 20 years later, when Paul wrote to the Corinthians. The kerygma itself involves referential claims about certain narrated events. Even the creed, with its reference to Jesus' crucifixion under Pontius Pilate, takes pains to locate the event of Jesus' death on the stage of world history. The Gospel is not only the offer of a new self-understanding; rather, it is a proclamation that certain events happened among flesh-and-blood people in history and that somehow these events have wrought a fundamental transformation in our relationship to God. That's why the Gospels take the form they do. They are not timeless teachings; they are not mystical revelations from Heaven; they are not celebrations of the author's own personal relationship with Jesus; rather, they are history-like narratives. So that's the first point as to why we should care: the character of the witnesses themselves.

The question of truth. The second point, closely linked, is the question of truth. We pursue historical inquiry because of our own innate, God-given, God-driven desire to know the truth.

Intellectual integrity demands it. We're not just play-acting, living in some imaginary magic kingdom of Disney Bibleland. This doesn't mean, as the Jesus Seminar supposes, that we have to tailor the content of Christian preaching to include only what a historian accepts, but it does mean we want to know whether the Gospel we preach is somehow continuous with events that happened in real space-time history, and whether this preaching is in some sense faithful to those events or whether it is simply fantasy. Of course, historical evidence can never prove the truth of the Gospel. Even if the narrative of Jesus' death and resurrection is historically factual, that doesn't prove that these events occurred for us and for our salvation. That's a different matter to interpret the significance of those events in that way. But if the referential claims are fundamentally false, then as Paul says, "We are of all people most to be pitied." We are living a lie, and the whole thing has to be seen as a pious fiction, as human aspiration writ large. It's no longer outside ourselves, but rather we become subject to the charges of Feuerbach and Freud, that the Gospel is simply wishful thinking, the projection of our human hopes and needs.

What I am saying is that historical investigation cannot prove the truth of the Gospel, but it might disprove it. Why then do it? Because otherwise our preaching and our faith become un-checked ideology. By pressing the question about the Jesus of history, we seek to avoid falling into a sentimental morass of religious subjectivity that ignores the question of what God has actually done in the world. As Leander Keck has argued, the historical inquiry then has the effect of interrogating our religious convictions and allowing the Jesus of history to pose questions to us, questions to the image of him that the church builds up over time. Thus, our attempt at historical reflection, speaking from within the church, stands in a dialectical cross-checking relation with our confessional traditions. As Anselm formulated it (speaking not about the historical Jesus but about other matters), it's a question of faith seeking understanding.

Internal logic of Christian doctrine. I will make three points about the way in which the internal logic of Christian doctrine requires this historical inquiry. First, the doctrine of incarnation: if Jesus of Nazareth was a real human being who lived in a particular place—Galilee and Judaea in the first century—then his life may be investigated historically in precisely the same way as the life of any other human being, whether Socrates, Julius Caesar, Martin Luther, or Martin Luther King, Jr. It does not follow that historical investigation can tell us everything we want to know about Jesus. Far from it; the sources are too limited. But in principle there is nothing inappropriate about the investigation. If that is not true, if we claim that Jesus is some-how beyond the scope of historical inquiry, are we not falling unwittingly into Docetism, that is, denying that he was a real human being? The Christ of faith *is* the Jesus of history, Jesus of Nazareth; so the Apostles proclaimed, so the church has insisted. That is the scandal of the particularity of the Incarnation.

Let me put the question this way: does it in fact matter if Jesus of Nazareth was dragged kicking and screaming against his will to the cross? Does it? It seems to me that Johnson would have to answer, in principle, "No, it doesn't matter; what matters is the way the story is told in the Gospel proclamation." But there *is* something more at stake in the particularity of Jesus' humanity. It does matter that the flesh-and-blood man, Jesus, lived the obedience of faith—obedience even unto death on a cross—because his example teaches us that to trust in the power of God is not to trust in vain.

The second point about the internal logic of Christian doctrine concerns the eschatological reservation. Johnson seems to affirm that Jesus can be known in a fully satisfactory way through his presence in the church now. Of course, there are precedents of this view in the New Testament, particularly the Gospel of John. But this seems to me to be a one-sided account of the New Testament witness, which also insists that we do not yet see him as we desire, that we walk by faith, not by sight. Alongside John, we have the Gospel of Mark, whose glad tidings conclude with the mysterious figure at the tomb saying to the women, "He is risen, he is not here." We have a foretaste in the Spirit, but we do not enjoy his unmediated presence. That's why the popular language that one hears in some forms of evangelical Christianity about having a personal relationship with Jesus—language which, by the way, is entirely unbiblical—strikes us as glib and disingenuous. It simply does not do justice to the New Testament's eschatological reservation—the awareness of the "not yet," the insistence that we hope for what we do not see. In this eschatological interval, our hope must take its bearings in a significant way from what has been given us in the historical past.

The third point concerning the internal logic of Christian doctrine concerns the significance of the people Israel. One important aspect of the story of Jesus in the Gospels is that Jesus lived and died as a Jew. His teachings were deeply grounded in Israel's traditions and his hope for the future was inextricably interwoven with the fate of the people Israel. One glaring error of the Jesus Seminar crowd is that they drive a wedge between Jesus and Jewish culture. That is simply bad history and it could also have disastrous theological and practical consequences. The last equally sustained effort to portray an un-Jewish Jesus was undertaken by the theologians of the Third Reich. But I'm worried that, in a more subtle way, even Johnson's approach will lead us away from the Jewishness of Jesus and the significance of Israel. If all we need to know about Jesus we learned in the Christian liturgy or in the experience of our own prayer lives, then the ties of this Jesus to his people, a particular people distant from us in time and culture, may become increasingly tenuous. And the end product of this is a Jesus who is a Christian. That, in fact, is a dangerous distortion, and has been a demonstrable phenomenon in the history of the church. So there's much to be gained theologically by insisting on seeing Jesus in his first-century Jewish historical context. In order to illustrate that, I want to turn from my rebuttal to Johnson and discuss the contributions of N.T. Wright.

I assume that many of you will be acquainted, at least to some degree, with Wright's work. Wright is a British New Testament scholar who taught for a time at McGill University in Montreal. He later returned to England, where he became chaplain at Worcester College and lecturer in New Testament at Oxford. More recently, he has become the dean of Lichfield Cathedral in England. His much awaited book, *Jesus and the Victory of God*, appeared last year. In this book, he takes on the question of the Jesus of history and challenges us to rethink everything we thought we knew. I want to consider with you how this book might be pertinent for our consideration of New Testament ethics, although Wright himself actually does not address this question directly in the book. My comments will be broken into four parts. First, I will sketch the overall contours of Wright's portrait of the historical Jesus. Second, I offer some focused observations pertinent to the question of ethics within Wright's portrait. Third, I list briefly a few points where I think Wright's construction is open to critique. Finally, I offer reflections on the significance of this particular construction of the historical Jesus for New Testament ethics.

First, Wright's portrayal of Jesus. This is a bold, sweeping proposal that tries to integrate the data of the Gospel traditions in a fresh and surprising way and to stand against the stream of much current historical Jesus research. The people in the Jesus Seminar group have portrayed Jesus as a wandering Cynic philosopher who went around spouting mysterious aphorisms. In their view, he didn't have any particular religious or political program, and he didn't have any sense of himself as being a unique figure; nor did he have any eschatological or apocalyptic expectations for the future. Wright, on the other hand, insists that we have to understand Jesus as a first-century Jewish apocalyptic prophet. Jesus came proclaiming the kingdom of God, by which he meant several things: he meant, first of all, the restoration of Israel from exile. This is one of the surprising points about Wright's construction. He argues that even though first-century Jews were living in the land of Israel and had the

Temple intact, nonetheless, they thought of themselves as still being in exile, because they were still under the thumb of foreign oppressors and client rulers. Yahweh had not come triumphantly to restore the Davidic monarchy—so they were still in exile. Second, according to Wright, this proclamation of the kingdom of God entailed the claim that God was about to act or was in fact now acting to bring about the final triumph over the powers of evil and human suffering. And third, as an integral part of this, the proclamation of the kingdom of God meant that Yahweh was about to return to Zion and manifest his glory.

Jesus believed, Wright argues, that all of this was taking place in and through his own ministry. In other words, Jesus did not come teaching people how to go to Heaven when they die; Jesus did not come proclaiming some future cosmic event that would bring about the end of the space-time universe. Instead, Wright takes all of the apocalyptic language in the Gospels and reinterprets it as coded language referring to specific historical events that Jesus believed would happen in the near future, in the lifetime of himself and his immediate followers. Here Wright is following very closely Albert Schweitzer's classic reconstruction of the historical Jesus.

This message, that Jesus came proclaiming, had two quite distinct prongs to it. It was a glad and joyous message of hope and restoration and comfort, welcome to sinners who could at last be received into this coming Kingdom; but at the same time it carried a warning of imminent catastrophe: if Israel did not change its ways, divine judgment would come upon them. Wright argues that Jesus ought to be understood as being just like the Old Testament prophets, like Amos and Jeremiah, proclaiming that a great disaster would befall the unfaithful nation Israel. Notice how this portrayal of Jesus places him on the ground in the context of the political and religious history of first-century Judaism. It also makes clear, in Wright's reconstruction, that Jesus was engaged in a powerful critique of first-century Judaism.

The main elements of this critique, as I understand them in

Wright's construction, are these: First of all, Jesus criticized Judaism because of its narrowness, its insistence on clinging to election as a matter of privilege and acting in a manner that was hostile and heedless toward the pagan world. This behavior was a betrayal of that for which God had destined Israel, namely, to be a light to the nations, as we read in Isaiah. Wright believes that this was Jesus' view of the matter. Second, the disastrous course that Israel was on had to do with their commitment to nationalism and violence. On Wright's reconstruction, the revolutionary resistance movement against Roman rule was a powerful force bubbling up throughout first-century Judaism. Wright argues that even the Pharisees, though they are not portrayed this way in the Gospels, were also committed to programs of national revolutionary zealot violence. Against all of this Jesus came proclaiming a new way of being the people of God, a new construal of Israel's worldview symbols. Jesus, according to Wright, attacked what had become the standard symbols of the second-temple Jewish worldview, particularly on the issues of Sabbath, food laws, and worship in the temple—all of which were signs of the exclusivity that Jesus was criticizing.

There is a very long last part of the book where Wright discusses Jesus' aims and beliefs, what we would call Jesus' own self-interpretation.[5] Wright argues that Jesus was enacting in his own person, in his final journey to Jerusalem, these elements of return from exile, defeat of evil, and the return of Yahweh to Zion. He believed he was the Messiah, and that "the fortunes of the people were drawn together onto himself and his own work."[6] When Jesus went to Jerusalem for his final confrontation with the authorities, he undertook three great symbolic actions. The first is the turning over of the tables and driving the money-changers out of the temple. Wright interprets this as an act of judgment, God's judgment prefiguring the destruction of the whole system of temple worship. The second great symbolic action is the Last Supper, which symbolizes the enactment of a new exodus, a new coming to freedom and manifestation of the delivering power of God. Then, finally, in a complex argument,

Wright argues that Jesus' action of going to the cross is itself a prophetic, symbolic action, which Jesus knowingly and deliberately undertook as a way of enacting, in his person, God's judgment on the unfaithful people Israel and, at the same time, bringing about the final defeat of the power of evil.

That is a very quick sketch of Wright's lengthy and complex construction. In the context of that overall sketch, I want to offer some specific observations pertinent to ethics. The section that is most relevant to our concerns appears in the part of the book where Wright is outlining the message that Jesus proclaimed, in a chapter called "Stories of the Kingdom: Invitation, Welcome, Challenge and Summons." An excerpt at the beginning of that chapter gives an overview of the way in which Wright sees Jesus' proclamation as pertinent to the question of ethics.

> Jesus' . . . kingdom narratives carried as part of their story-line the sense that his hearers were invited to see themselves as the Israel who would benefit from his work; and also, to some extent at least, as the "helpers" who would have an active share in that work. With that invitation, there went a further implication: the returned-from-exile Israel must conduct itself in a certain fashion. Nor was this simply a general set of rules, a new abstract "ethic." The unique and unrepeatable nature of Jesus' own sense of vocation extended to those who followed him. They were summoned to specific tasks which had to do with his own career and project. The *story* of the kingdom thus generated an appropriate *praxis* among those who heard it and made it their own. . . . Jesus' appeals, commands, and so forth are to be seen not simply as "new teaching" in the sense of a few new moral rules or theological principles, but as part of the underlying story he told, which aimed to produce in his hearers a realignment of their own praxis, necessarily involving a realignment of the other elements of their worldview also.[7]

That quotation, particularly the last part of it, has some interesting echoes of what I was saying earlier about ethics being grounded less in rules and principles than in stories and symbolic worldviews. Something very similar to that is what Wright wants to argue about the nature Jesus' program and the claim that it made on his followers.

Out of Wright's lengthy discussion of this kingdom practice and worldview, I want to lift out five salient points that are of interest for our questions about New Testament ethics.

First, Jesus clearly understood himself to be calling and forming a community. He was gathering what Wright calls "cells" of followers. Unlike the Essenes who withdrew into the caves at Qumran to live a separated life, they were living in the midst of the people, nonetheless they were "cells" of a gathered community living in a distinctive way as the alternative new Israel which was defined particularly by their allegiance to Jesus.

A second point: the character of this community was that it was a new covenant community; therefore, it was characterized by the renewed heart, a changed heart. In accordance with the new covenant promise of Jeremiah 31 the law was to be written on their hearts, and one implication of this is that they were to enact forgiveness among themselves. An important piece of evidence for Wright's argument is Jesus' prohibition of divorce. Notice what he says to the people that are interrogating him: "Yes, right, we know that Deuteronomy 24 allows divorce, but Moses gave you that law because of the hardness of your hearts. But it's not to be so now" (see Mark 10:4–5). So Jesus is proclaiming a new state of affairs among his followers where hardness of heart no longer prevails, but where the people of the new covenant are given new hearts.

Third, this new covenant people is not to make common cause with the resistance movement. Instead, they are called to the way of creative nonviolent resistance. This is a major theme that Wright hammers home again and again, that they are not to engage in the ultimately self-destructive effort to revolt against Roman authority.

Fourth, these people are called to live by the jubilee principle among themselves. Within these little "cell" communities they are called to forgive economic debts and to pool resources.

Fifth, this community is to be a light to the world. Jesus envisioned the redrawing of Israel's boundaries so that these communities would become a light to the Gentiles and reach out to the world as the Old Testament prophets had envisioned that God's glory would do. Jesus believed that after his death, this community would go on, and here I quote, "implementing what he had achieved by becoming Isaianic heralds—lights to the world." Their witness had to be not just in words, but through actions, in praxis. For those who would follow Jesus, "The aim is not simply to believe as many true things as possible, but to act in obedience, implementing the achievement of Jesus while spurred and sustained by true belief."[8]

Time permits me to offer only a few points of critique of this picture of the historical Jesus and his program. I will list four points, without going into any detail about them, where I think that Wright's overall construction is open to challenge, historically speaking.

First, did first-century Jews, in fact, generally understand themselves to be in exile? It seems to me that Wright has overstated his case on this point. Certainly, they hoped for a radical eschatological intervention of God. They still hoped for a radical renewal, but it's not clear to me that one can make the case that they thought they were in exile. Certainly the Qumran community, out there in the caves at the Dead Sea, thought that they were in exile, but whether that was characteristic of Judaism more broadly and whether that's what Jesus thought, I'm not yet convinced by Wright's discussion.

Second, Wright's reinterpretation of eschatology and of Jewish apocalyptic language tends to focus on the claim that Jesus fulfilled everything through his death and resurrection, and it leads to the virtual evaporation of any element of future hope in Christian proclamation. Wright has done a great deal of very provocative exegetical work to support this case, but it seems to me that, on the whole, he fails to account for the pervasive future-oriented eschatological expectation in early Christianity, including the expectation of a future resurrection of the dead, which also nearly disappears from Wright's reconstruction of Jesus and his teaching. So he is left with the problem of how to understand the fact that the world continues and that evil continues. He himself sees this near the end of the book. He writes movingly about it as follows: "The real problem is this: Jesus interpreted his coming death and the vindication he expected after that death as the defeat of evil, but, on the first Easter Monday, evil still stalked the earth from Jerusalem to Gibraltar and beyond and stalks it still."[9] Wright's way of reconstructing Jesus leaves us in a very difficult position, and we find it very hard to provide an answer to that problem, because he essentially has a realized eschatology. It's not an accident, by the way, that he was a student of George Caird at Oxford who in turn had been a student of C.H. Dodd, the greatest proponent of realized eschatology among twentieth-century New Testament scholars.

A third point of critique: Wright may exaggerate the degree to which Jesus' contemporaries, especially the Pharisees, were committed to a program of violent revolution. This is a very controversial historical point, and many people are strongly skeptical of the way that Wright reads the evidence on this point. If he is wrong about it, then it is harder to place as much emphasis as he does on Israel's espousal of violence as the central cause for God's judgment upon Israel.

The fourth point of critique is that the last section of the book on Jesus' aims and beliefs attributes to Jesus an extremely elaborate and full-blown interpretation of his own death in terms of Old Testament prophetic images and typologies. Actually, I am sympathetic to that move, but the construction is at least vulnerable because of its extreme complexity; it involves a lot of conjectural moves that most historians would find hard to follow. It is easier to believe, many people think, that these complicated prophetic typological interpretations emerged over time, after the fact, as the early church tried to reflect about the significance of Jesus' death.

Finally, let me offer some comments on the overall significance of Wright's account for our understanding of New
Testament ethics. I want to make four positive comments, then
end by raising two questions.

First, Wright's construction of the historical Jesus does a
great service for New Testament ethics by stressing the theme of
continuity with Israel and Israel's heritage. If Jesus' activity
pointed toward the creation of a restored Israel proleptically
figured in the community of his disciples, then we as the church
need to maintain the continuity of our life and witness with the
historical Jesus and thereby with Israel. Our identity ought to be
grounded in the traditions of Israel, and we must continue to
wrestle with issues posed by Israel's election and Israel's
unfaithfulness. The struggle with this tension between Israel's
election and Israel's unfaithfulness was central to Jesus' career,
and it must remain central for the church. In my book, *Moral
Vision of the New Testament*, I have devoted a lengthy chapter
(chapter 17) to the problem of the church's attitude toward
Judaism as an ethical issue, and I think Wright's work supports
the importance of that undertaking.

The second point where I think Wright has made a contribution is in his highlighting Jesus' critique of violence. In Wright's
construction, this is absolutely central to Jesus' message and
mission. It is not simply a matter of a few sayings sprinkled
among others ("turn the other cheek" and so on). Instead, Jesus'
whole critique of Israel has to do with their adopting the ways of
pagan violence. Following is just one passage where he says this
forcefully,

> Jesus denounced, as no better than pagans, not only those
> who compromised with Caesar by playing his power games,
> *but also those who compromised with him by thinking to
> defeat him with his own weapons.* . . .His kingdom-an-
> nouncement, like all truly Jewish kingdom-announcements,
> came as the message of the one true God, the God of Israel,
> in opposition to pagan power, pagan gods, and pagan
> politics. But, unlike the other kingdom-announcers of his

> time from Judas the Galilean to Simeon Ben Kosiba, Jesus
> declared that the way of the kingdom was the way of peace,
> the way of love, the way of the cross. Fighting the battle of
> the kingdom with the enemy's weapons meant that one had
> already lost it, in principle, and would soon lose it, and lose
> it terribly, in practice.[10]

This is integral to Wright's portrait of Jesus and, to the extent
that this becomes a historically persuasive account, I would hope
that it might move the church more broadly to give fuller
consideration to the importance of Jesus' renunciation of
violence.

A third point: anchoring Jesus' concerns in real world history
is integral to Wright's project. According to Wright, the future
that Jesus envisioned is not an other-worldly destiny in heaven
abstracted from this world, but it is a concrete political future for
the people Israel in a continuing life on this earth. It seems to me
that, in this respect as in others, Wright's program is profoundly
congruent with the sketch in John Howard Yoder's book, *The
Politics of Jesus*.[11] Interestingly, Wright does not seem to discuss
Yoder or interact with him very much. Nonetheless, I think this
is a significant convergence, and it would be an interesting
question to pursue. The point is, according to Wright, that the
victory of God is to be implemented in human community; it is
not something that happens in some otherworldly sphere.

Fourth, the community of Jesus' followers is to be characterized by a strong sense of communal life; they are to be forgiving,
share goods, reach across ethnic and national boundaries, and of
course be a nonviolent community. I find this focus on community to be important and profoundly congenial. It is also a very
important corrective to the silly picture of Jesus as a wandering
philosopher who didn't care anything about community.

Now, my two concluding questions for Wright: What about
the cross? In my book, I write, "Jesus of Nazareth died on a
cross. Those who follow him could hardly expect better treatment from the world. Insofar as the community of faith follows
the path of the Jesus of history, it should expect suffering as its

lot."[12] But what does Wright's account of Jesus' understanding of his vocation do to my proposal about the image of the cross as an ethical paradigm? Does Wright's portrayal make the cross a one-time event of obedience for Jesus only, focused on one distinct historical moment of crisis, so that Jesus in his person enacts God's judgment and God's victory, exempting others from suffering? Wright's discussion in this book is not very clear about that point.

My final question is this: More generally, how does this specific historical agenda of Jesus which Wright sketches relate to what we are called to do today? It seems clear that Wright wants to argue that the teachings of Jesus in the Gospels are not timeless, general moral admonitions. Rather, they are particular directives for Israel at a particular moment of historical crisis. My question is: how do we get from there to here? Wright hasn't told us. There is no explicit hermeneutical dimension to this book. In fairness to him, I should tell you that this book is only part two of a projected six-part series of volumes on early Christianity, and I do think he intends to get to this question eventually, but he has not done it yet.

Still, Wright has given us some clues, and here is my hunch, as I read him: story is the key. Those of us who live now, even many generations later, continue to live out the next act of the drama, as he puts it, "implementing the achievement of Jesus as heralds who bear witness to the story through obedient action." If that is correct, it means that we don't necessarily do exactly what Jesus did, but that we have to carry on this story. If that is correct, Wright's account of the historical Jesus proves, in the end, deeply congenial to my proposal that New Testament ethics necessarily involves metaphor-making, necessarily involves a continual retelling of the story by our own lives which correspond, in an indirect but analogical way, to the character of the New Testament stories. The question for us, then, becomes this: How do we form the life of our communities so that we carry on the story of return from exile, the story of a restored alternative Israel, and the story of the "Victory of God?"

Notes

1. Luke Timothy Johnson, "Why Scripture Isn't Enough," *Commonweal* (June 6, 1997): 24.

2. Harry T. Cook, "Bible Wisdom: An Exchange," *The Christian Century* 114 (April 23–30, 1997): 133.

3. Luke T. Johnson, *The Real Jesus: The Misguided Quest for the Historical Jesus and the Truth of the Traditional Gospels* (San Francisco: Harper San Francisco, 1996), 133.

4. N.T. Wright, *Jesus and the Victory of God, vol. 2: Christian Origins and the Question of God* (Minneapolis: Augsburg Fortress, 1997).

5. Ibid., 475–653.

6. Ibid., 481.

7. Ibid., 245.

8. Ibid., 660.

9. Ibid., 659.

10. Ibid., 595.

11. John Howard Yoder, *The Politics of Jesus,* 2d ed (Grand Rapids, Eerd-mans, 1994).

12. Richard B. Hays, *The Moral Vision of the New Testament,* 167.

4

MALE AND FEMALE

A TEST CASE FOR METAPHORICAL METHOD

Now before faith came, we were imprisoned and guarded under law until faith would be revealed. Therefore the law was our disciplinarian until Christ came so that we might be justified by faith. But now that faith has come, we are no longer subject to a disciplinarian, for in Jesus Christ you are all children of God through faith. As many of you as were baptized into Christ, have clothed yourselves with Christ. There is no longer Jew or Greek, there is no longer slave or free, there is no longer male and female; for all of you are one in Christ Jesus. And if you belong to Christ, then you are Abraham's offspring, heirs according to the promise (Galatians 3:23–29).

In this lecture I will speak about the question of male and female in Christ as a test issue for the method, the approach to New Testament ethics, that I have been proposing and that I laid out in a schematic fashion in the second of these lectures. I don't know what it's like here, but where I come from, no issue is fraught with more tension than the politics of the relationship between men and women—not only in the culture generally but in the church, in particular. Just a couple of weeks ago in the United States we had, as you probably heard, an enormous rally in Washington DC of the "Promise Keepers"—a group of men gathering together to make pledges to keep their promises and be more responsible as Christian husbands and fathers to their family. You would think that sort of gesture might be welcomed, but in fact it was highly controversial. Many feminist groups find the Promise Keepers a very threatening group. The feminists fear that Promise Keepers will promote abusive male authority in

Christian households. I just mention that as one recent political event that has once again highlighted the ongoing difficult debate about how we, as women and men, are to relate to one another. On this issue, we are in great need of careful reflection about the way that the Bible might inform our common life. I think we have to face it: we are broken and confused and, in many cases, in need of healing. Part of the problem when we come to confront a question like this is that we are formed as men and women with very different sensibilities. Whether that is a matter of being formed by nature, or whether it's a matter of being shaped by culture, it comes out in all sorts of ways that touch our lives daily.

Just as one illustration of the sort of thing I mean, I've chosen an excerpt from a column by Dave Barry. The title of this column is "Listen Up Jerks, Share Innermost Feelings With Her." Here's what Barry writes:

> We have some good friends, Buzz and Libby, whom we see about twice a year. When we get together my wife Beth and Libby always wind up in a conversation lasting several days, during which they discuss virtually every significant event that has occurred in their lives and the lives of those they care about—sharing their innermost feelings, analyzing and probing, inevitably coming to a deeper understanding of each other and a strengthening of cherished relationships. Whereas Buzz and I watch the play-offs. This is not to say Buzz and I don't share our feelings. Sometimes we get quite emotional. "That's not a foul!"one of us will say, or "You're telling me that's not a foul?" I don't mean to suggest that all we talk about is sports. We also discuss, openly and without shame, what kind of pizza we need to order. We have a fine time, but we don't have heavy conversations. And sometimes, after the visit is over, I'm surprised to learn, from Beth, who learned it from Libby, that there's recently been some new wrinkle in Buzz's life, such as that he now has an artificial leg.

Well, it sounds like my house; I don't know about yours.

That is part of the problem, but that's only part of it. Some argue that the Bible itself is a source of the problem, that the Bible contains texts that are in fact nothing short of abusive, texts that oppress women, that even underwrite violence against women. Dr. Stephen Barton, who teaches New Testament at the University of Durham, England, recently sent me a new book he's published entitled, *Invitation to the Bible.*[1] The first chapter of this book, which is intended as an introduction for undergraduates, is entitled, "Hate Mail or Love-Letter: What Kind of Book is the Bible and What is it For?"[2] It's quite extraordinary, I think, that the Bible can be construed as hate mail. But some in our culture and some within the church, at least in the United States, are making such claims about the Bible.

I want us to look carefully now at the evidence, the biblical teachings on the relation between men and women. Although our time is limited, I will sketch out how complex this picture is. I believe that this is one of these issues on which we do find internal tensions within the canon. Scripture does not teach a single, univocal perspective as we try to look at these matters, so we need to try to think our way through it. I might as well be honest and tell you that this is what I am trying to do, both as an academic exercise and in trying to sort out what this means for my own life of discipleship. So this is an experimental run. This is not one of the questions I treated in my book, *Moral Vision of the New Testament;* this is one that I avoided in that book. So in this lecture I will run a number of things by you and I hope to learn from your readings and responses as well.

I will begin by looking briefly not at a New Testament text, but at Genesis 1 and 2, a couple of passages that are foundational for several of the New Testament texts we will be looking at later. These texts—the Genesis creation narratives—have been very important historically in the church's discussion of the relationship between male and female.

The first one is the creation account in Genesis 1: "God said, 'Let us make humankind in our image, according to our

likeness; and let them have dominion over the fish of the sea.'.
.. So God created human kind in his image, in the image of God
he created them; male and female he created them. God blessed
them, and God said to them, 'Be fruitful and multiply and fill the
earth and subdue it; and have dominion . . .'" (Genesis 1:26a,
27–28a). In this text we have the creation of male and female
equally in the image of God; they equally bear the *imago dei*.
This is part of God's blessing on creation. In Genesis 2, of
course, we have a further account that begins to complicate
things a bit. In verse 18 we see the man is created first: "The
Lord God said, 'It is not good that the man should be alone: I
will make him a helper as his partner.' . . ." And God brings all
of the animals and so on, but this is not adequate. God causes a
sleep to fall on the man and takes a rib out, makes it into a
woman, and brings her to the man. Then the man said, "This at
last is bone of my bones and flesh of my flesh; this one shall be
called Woman, for out of Man this one was taken. Therefore a
man leaves his father and mother and clings to his wife, and they
become one flesh. And the man and his wife were both naked
and were not ashamed" (2:23–25).

This is followed by the account of the temptation and
disobedience of Adam and Eve. The last verse I want to draw
your attention to is the conclusion of the curse that is pronounced by God upon the woman after this disobedience. He
says, "I will greatly increase your pangs in childbearing; in pain
you shall bring forth children, yet your desire shall be for your
husband, and he shall rule over you" (3:16). The man is given
other curses to bear: having to earn his bread by the sweat of his
face and, indeed, finally the curse of death. The statement that
the husband shall rule over the woman is in the text of the Bible,
but it is part of the punishment that falls upon Adam and Eve as
a result of their disobedience; it is not part of the original created
order. That point becomes very important later on as we consider
the New Testament understanding of this text.

With that in the background, I want to turn to some of the
New Testament texts. This will be all too hasty a survey. If we

were really doing this right, if I were writing this as a chapter in my book, I would give you 50 or 60 pages of mind-numbingly detailed exegesis about each of these passages, but we are simply going to have to look at them quickly.

Subordination of Women. First I want to look at a collection of texts that teach or command or in some way presuppose the subordination of women and/or wives. I will take these in canonical order. The first one is in 1 Corinthians 11:2–3. Paul writes to the Corinthians, "I commend you because you remember me in everything and maintain the traditions just as I handed them onto you. But I want you to understand that Christ is the head of every man, and the husband is the head of his wife." In Greek there are no specific words for "husband" and "wife." In the Greek text we find simply the words "man" and "woman," and if you are following in another translation, it might very well rightly say, "the man is the head of the woman" rather than "the husband is the head of his wife." There is no indication here that Paul is talking about married couples. I think it is probably a more generic statement: Christ is the head of every man, the man is the head of the woman, God is the head of Christ.

Then in 11:5ff he goes on into a puzzling passage about women who pray and prophesy in the assembly with their heads uncovered or unveiled. This passage is full of exegetical problems and difficulties and things that no one really understands, particularly the odd statement in verse 10 that a woman ought to have authority on her head "because of the angels." There is no explanation given in the text of what that means. Exegetes have offered all kinds of speculations, but they remain exactly that, speculations. The main thing I want to call to your attention about this text is, first of all, that it does create what looks like a cosmic ontological hierarchy: God, Christ, man, woman. That has something to do with Paul's insistence that women ought to keep their heads covered somehow when they pray in worship. I will come back to this text later, but it is already worth noting that Paul does assume that women *will* pray and prophesy publicly in the assembly. It is a question of what symbolic covering they have on their heads; it may not be a covering even, but rather a matter of having their hair bound up appropriately. This is another hotly debated question.

Moving on to 1 Corinthians 14:34–35, we find these instructions: "Women should be silent in the churches. For they are not permitted to speak, but should be subordinate, as the law also says. If there is anything they desire to know, let them ask their husbands at home. For it is shameful for a woman to speak in church." That text hardly requires any comment: it clearly calls for women to be silent and subjugated and subordinate to their husbands. The interesting thing, though, is that we have a text critical problem here. That is, there is room for reasonable doubt whether these sentences belong in the letter that Paul originally wrote to the Corinthians. A number of recent commentators, including Gordon Fee in his very extensive critical commentary on 1 Corinthians,[3] have argued that in fact these verses are an interpolation, that they were added to the text at some later stage by someone who edited or compiled the text. There are signs in a number of ancient Greek manuscripts that these verses are marked as a gloss or as somehow not belonging to the text. The thing that makes that an especially appealing theory about the original form of the text is that if you look at the rest of the chapter as a whole, it is all about the exercise of tongues and prophecy and whether prophets can speak and so on; if you remove verses 34 and 35, which are precisely the two verses marked in some ancient manuscripts, the text reads very smoothly. Paul says:

> Let two or three prophets speak, and let the others weigh what is said. If a revelation is made to someone else sitting nearby, let the first person be silent. For you can all prophesy one by one, so that all may learn and all be encouraged. And the spirits of prophets are subject to the prophets, for God is a God not of disorder, but of peace as in all the churches of the saints. . . . Or did the word of God originate with you? Or are you the only ones it has reached? Anyone

who claims to be a prophet, or to have spiritual powers, must acknowledge that what I'm writing to you is a command of the Lord (1 Corinthians 14: 29–33, 36–37).

You see how cleanly that reads? Verses 34 and 35 look like an interruption inserted by a second hand at a later point. The other evidence which supports that view is that Paul has just said, three chapters earlier, that when women pray and prophesy in the worship service, they have to have their heads covered. So what sense would it make for him to say three chapters later that they are to be utterly silent and that it's shameful for a woman to speak in church? My own view is that these two verses are a secondary addition to the text

It doesn't solve our problems to say that, but it is helpful in understanding what was going on in first-century Christianity. All of the other evidence of Paul's letters seems to suggest that women played active roles in the leadership of worship. So these verses are a little odd, to say the least.

Let's move on to the next text in Ephesians 5: "Wives be subject to your husbands as you are to the Lord. For the husband is the head of the wife just as Christ is head of the church, the body of which he is the Savior. Just as the church is subject to Christ, so also wives ought to be, in everything, to their husbands" (v. 22–24). This is of course one of a series called household codes (*Haustafeln*) in the New Testament. There is one here, one in Colossians (3:18–19), and another one in 1 Peter (3:1–7). Each of these texts gives a whole list of directions about servants being subject to masters, children to parents, and wives to husbands. Of course, these are very conventional ideas in the ancient world, not just in the New Testament, as Professor David Schroeder has demonstrated in some of his earlier scholarly work.[4] However, the thing that is unusual about Ephesians 5:22–33 is that it doesn't tell the husband to rule the wife strictly. Instead, the word is addressed to the wife to be subordinate to the husband.

There's a similar passage in Colossians 3:18–19. We will not look at that one now, but let's consider the one in 1 Peter 3:

> Wives, in the same way, accept the authority of your husbands, so that even if some of them do not obey the word, they may be won over without a word by their wives' conduct, when they see the purity and reverence of your lives. Do not adorn yourself outwardly by braiding your hair, wearing gold ornaments or fine clothing; rather, let your adornment be the inner self with the lasting beauty of a gentle and quiet spirit (1 Peter 3:1–4).

Then in verse 7 it turns and addresses the husbands, "In the same way show consideration for your wives in your life together, paying honor to the woman as the weaker sex, since they too are also heirs of the gracious gift of life—so that nothing may hinder your prayers " (see also Titus 2:3–5.).

The last passage that certainly must be looked at in this connection is 1 Timothy 2:8–15. I pick it up in verse 11, which is where the rubber hits the road:

> Let a woman learn in silence with full submission. I permit no woman to teach or have authority over a man; she is to keep silent. For Adam was formed first, then Eve; and Adam was not deceived, but the woman was deceived and became a transgressor. [An odd reading of Genesis 2!] Yet she will be saved through childbearing, provided they continue in faith and love and holiness, with modesty (1 Timothy 2:11–15).

On this one, there is no text critical problem. This is clearly in the text of 1 Timothy in the canonical New Testament. The passage unequivocally forbids women to teach or have authority and grounds that in the fact that Eve was first deceived by the serpent. That is the classic collection of New Testament texts on the subordination of women.

Women in Leadership. Next I want to look at a second category of texts. These, also taken from the New Testament epistles, depict women in roles of ministry or leadership in the community. First we go to Romans 16: "I commend to you our sister

Phoebe, a deacon of the church at Cenchreae, so that you may welcome her in the Lord as is fitting for the saints, and help her in whatever she may require from you, for she has been a benefactor of many and of myself as well" (16:1–2). The translation I read here, "Phoebe, a *deacon* of the church," is a certainly a correct translation. The Greek word is *diakonos*. Some older texts translated this as deaconess, as though it were a feminine variant of the form, but it is not. It describes Phoebe simply as a "deacon" of the church. Whether that actually means an ecclesiastical office or whether it simply means "servant" is a debated question. *Diakonos* is the ordinary word that means servant. But when it says she has been a "benefactor," there the Greek word is *prostatis* ("one who stands before"). It is a word that is used of people who are in positions of authority and leadership in a community. Phoebe is the bearer of Paul's letter to Rome. She is delivering this letter to the community and is Paul's appointed spokesperson; this is his word of commendation for her, asking the church to do whatever she requires them to do.

Going on in Romans 16, we find a whole list of greetings, several of which are interesting for our present concerns. "Greet Prisca and Aquila, who work with me in Christ Jesus, and who risked their necks for my life, to whom not only I give thanks, but also all the churches of the Gentiles" (v.4). This is of course the married couple mentioned in Acts, where Prisca is also called Priscilla. It is unusual that the woman in the couple is listed first. This suggests that she is perhaps of higher social status than her husband, and it may mean that she is more of a leading figure. Continuing on down, jumping to verse 6: "Greet Mary, who has worked very hard among you. Greet Andronicus and Junia. . . ." If you have a text that says "Junias," that is just wrong. The name is a feminine one, Junia. The text was corrupted by some early copyists who added the masculine ending to it because they couldn't believe what the rest of the sentence says: "my relatives who were in prison with me; they are prominent among the apostles." This is clearly a woman named

Junia whom Paul is describing as being "among the apostles." Now of course Paul uses the term "apostle" differently from the way that Luke, for example, uses it. It's a word that simply means "one who is a missionary," commissioned by God to preach and proclaim the Gospel. Junia gets classed in that category. So here we have in Romans 16 a number of women who clearly are fellow workers with Paul in his apostolic mission. There is no indication that he regards them as anything other than full participants.

Of course, in Acts 18:24–26, we also have another reference to Priscilla and how she and Aquila took Apollos in hand and instructed him more correctly "in the things concerning Jesus and the Gospel." In Philippians 4, we have a mention of two women about whom we know nothing beyond what Paul says about them here. They are apparently having some sort of a disagreement between themselves at the time Paul writes this letter, and he says: "I urge Euodia and I urge Syntyche to be of the same mind in the Lord. Yes and I ask you also, my loyal companion, help these women, for they have struggled beside me in the work of the Gospel, together with Clement and the rest of my co-workers, whose names are in the book of life" (Philippians 4:2–3). When Paul uses this language about struggling alongside him in the work of the Gospel, this is quasi-technical language for describing the work of preaching the apostolic message. He does not simply mean that they went along and made the coffee. These are clearly women of some prominence in the church at Philippi, and Paul is concerned that the dispute between them be settled.

I include 1 Corinthians 11 in this category because it speaks of women praying in the community. The reference in Acts 21:9 is the reference to the daughters of Philip, who were prophets. Acts 16:11–15 is the story about Lydia, who, according to this story in Acts 16, apparently is a household head. When Paul arrives in Philippi and they go out to the place of prayer down by the river,

> A certain woman named Lydia, a worshiper of God, was
> listening to us; she was from the city of Thyatira and a
> dealer in purple cloth. The Lord opened her heart to listen
> eagerly to what was said by Paul. When she and her house-
> hold were baptized, she urged us, saying, "If you have
> judged me to be faithful to the Lord, come and stay at my
> home." And she prevailed upon us (Acts 16:14–15).

No mention here of a husband or a father; Lydia seems to be the
head of this household and is a prosperous merchant. She
becomes the first convert in Paul's preaching at Philippi.

To this list should be added Luke 24, which narrates the
important fact that women were the first witnesses to the
resurrection. This is a consistent tradition in all of the Gospels.
In Luke's story, when the women find the tomb empty, they run
back and tell it to the eleven and all of the rest: "Now it was
Mary Magdalene, Joanna, Mary the mother of James, and the
other women with them who told this to the apostles. But these
words seemed to them an idle tale, and they did not believe
them" (v.10–11). Take note: the apostles are not listening to the
women's testimony. This is repeated in verses 22–27, when the
travelers on the road to Emmaus explained that the women
reported the news and were not believed. So, there are a number
of passages that depict women in roles of ministry, leadership,
proclamation, witness.

Equality and Mutuality of Male and Female. Next we must
consider a group of texts that articulate or imply the eschatological equality of male and female in Christ and hold up a vision of
mutuality. Galatians 3:23–29 was quoted at the beginning of the
lecture. I want to say something about how it fits into the overall
argument of Galatians. Remember what Paul is arguing for in
this letter: that Gentiles do not have to be circumcised in order
to be incorporated fully into the community and to enjoy full
table fellowship with Gentiles. They are on equal ground and
equal footing. In support of that argument, he quotes here what
is probably an early baptismal tradition, that there is no longer

Jew nor Greek. The distinction between Jew and Greek ceases to be relevant in terms of their equal participation in the community. But then look what the other elements of the formula are: "no longer slave or free, and the [NRSV gets it right here] there is no longer male *and* female." Why do the first two say "no Jew *or* Greek, no slave *or* free" and why does it change to "*and*" in the third one? The answer is that the phrase is taken from Genesis 1:27 in the creation story: "God created them in his own image, male and female." So, the formula alludes to the creation story and says "no more." In other words Paul is saying, "new creation." There is a new creation, as in the hymn we sang tonight "new man, woman new." It's a whole new ball game. Among other things, this also certainly means that the curse pronounced on man and woman for their disobedience has now fallen on Christ, who became, it says in Galatians 3:13, "a curse for us." Those us of who are the recipients of God's grace through Christ are now empowered to live a new life in this new creation that is set free from the effects of the curse.

Let us consider another text, Acts 2. This is the Pentecost story. The people come around and say, "These people here who are speaking in tongues are all drunk." Peter says,

> No, this is what was spoken through the prophet Joel: "In the last days it will be, God declares, that I will pour out my Spirit upon *all flesh*, and your sons *and your daughters* shall prophesy, and your young men shall see visions, and your old men shall dream dreams. Even upon my slaves, *both men and women*, in those days I will pour out my Spirit; and they shall prophesy" (emphasis mine) (Acts 2:16–18).

This outpouring of the Spirit and the activity of prophecy is something in which male and female alike are expected to participate. Luke is probably especially happy to be able to quote the prophecy of Joel because it envisions both male and female participation in the new age of the Spirit.

In the next text, 1 Corinthians 7, Paul is writing to the Corinthians who, oddly enough, seem to have believed that now that they are Christians, married couples ought to stop having sex with each other. Paul says, "No, no you've got it all wrong." As he writes in 1 Corinthians 7:3–4, "The husband should give to his wife her conjugal rights, and likewise the wife to her husband. For the wife does not have authority over her own body, but the husband does; likewise the husband does not have authority over his own body, but the wife does." There is something new. What is interesting to me about this text is not only that it undercuts the unilateral authority of the husband over the wife and asserts a reciprocal authority of the wife over the husband, but also for us modern people, it doesn't support the notion of autonomy; it doesn't suggest that each individual has the right to control his or her own body. Instead, those who are in a marriage covenant relationship with one another have each surrendered authority to the other. There is a mutuality in that covenant relationship that is quite extraordinary in the context of the ancient world.

Lastly, back one more time to 1 Corinthians 11. I want to call attention to two verses I did not read before. After the discussion of hierarchy and veiling so that women can prophesy, Paul writes, "Nevertheless, in the Lord woman is not independent of man or man independent of woman. For just as woman came from man, so man comes through woman; but all things come from God" (v. 11–12). So even after insisting on the symbolism of sexual difference for women in the worship community, Paul, in a sense, undercuts it at the end, by saying that *in the Lord* there is a reciprocity of relationship where men and women each are dependent on the other.

Patriarchal Assumptions about Women. The final category is a group of narrative texts that subvert patriarchal assumptions about women. They overturn things in a surprising way. Matthew 15 includes the story of the Canaanite woman who comes asking for Jesus to heal her daughter. She says,

> ". . . my daughter is tormented by a demon." But he did not answer her at all. And his disciples came and urged him,

saying, "Send her away, for she keeps shouting after us." He answered, "I was sent only to the lost sheep of the house of Israel." But she came and knelt before him, saying, "Lord, help me." He answered, "It is not fair to take the children's food and throw it to the dogs" She said, "Yes, Lord, yet even the dogs eat the crumbs that fall from their masters' table." Then Jesus answered her, "Woman, great is your faith! Let it be done for you as you wish." And her daughter was healed instantly (Matthew 15:22b–28).

A colleague of mine, Gail O'Day, has written an article about this passage; the title is "Surprised by Faith."[5] Jesus is surprised. This is the only place in the Gospels where Jesus enters into a controversy dialogue and gets bested by somebody with a witty response that he cannot resist, not only because of the wit but because of her faith. She's both a woman and a Gentile (two strikes!); nonetheless, she gets what she requests from the Lord because of her persistence and her faith.

Mark 14 includes the story of a woman, who comes to anoint Jesus prior to the passion, in Bethany at the house of Simon the leper. She comes in and pours ointment on his head, and the disciples protest about this waste of money. Jesus says,

Let her alone; why do you trouble her? She has performed a good service for me. For you always have the poor with you, and you can show kindness to them whenever you wish; but you will not always have me. She has done what she could; she has anointed my body beforehand for its burial. Truly I tell you, wherever the good news is proclaimed in the whole world, what she has done will be told in remembrance of her (Mark 14:6–9).

Remember, this is in the context of Jesus being surrounded by wrong-headed, stupid disciples who keep not getting the point, who do not understand, who do not believe when Jesus tells them he is going to have to die. But this woman comes in, out of nowhere, as it were, and does understand and anoints him for burial. Thus, Jesus praises her.

Consider also the story of the Samaritan woman in John 4. Jesus meets the woman at the well and gets into a lengthy conversation with her. This story stands in stark contrast to the story of Nicodemus immediately before, the one who is a teacher of Israel and doesn't understand about Jesus. This Samaritan woman, through back and forth dialogue with Jesus, does indeed come to understand that he is Messiah and Christ. Jesus discloses himself to her and says,

> "I am he, the one who is speaking to you." Just then his disciples came. They were astonished that he was speaking with a woman, but no one said, "What do you want?" or "Why are you speaking with her?" Then the woman left her water jar and went back to the city. She said to the people, "Come and see a man who told me everything I have ever done! He cannot be the Messiah, can he?" They left the city and were on their way to him (John 4:26–30).

And in verse 39, we are told that: "Many Samaritans from that city believed in him because of the woman's testimony." So she becomes, as it were, an evangelist proclaiming the news that she has found in Jesus the Christ.

The last text in this category that I want to talk about, surprisingly, is Ephesians 5. Even though thispassage teaches that wives are to be subject to their husbands, it also contains other things that have to be considered if we are to be fair to this text. First of all, it begins in verse 21 by saying, "Be subject *to one another* out of reverence for Christ" (emphasis mine). Then we have in verses 22–24, the teaching about wives being subject. In verse 25, however, we get the address to the husbands:

> Husbands, love your wives, just as Christ loved the church and gave himself up for her, in order to make her holy by cleansing her with the washing of the water by the word, so as to present the church to himself in splendor, without a spot or wrinkle. . . . In the same way, husbands should love their wives as they do their own bodies. . . . For no one ever hates his own body, but he nourishes and tenderly cares for

it, just as Christ does for the church, because we are members of his body (Ephesians 5:25–30).

This is the part of the text that doesn't get quoted enough, but
the bite of moral exhortation in this passage is this word
addressed to the husband: the husbands are to take on the role of
Christ, which means taking on the role of servant. The role of
Christ in relation to the church is as one who serves, the one who
washes feet. That is what husbands are called to do in relation to
their wives. So clearly this is not a model that advocates domi-
nance, subjugation, and *certainly* not abuse of the wife. The
husband is to show tender care for her analogous to that of
Christ for the church.

This has been a very hasty survey of these texts. I suggest that
we ought to read them through the three focal images of community, cross, and new creation.

Community. It's clear that men and women are called to
participate in the community as, in the words of 1 Peter 3:7,
"joint heirs of the gracious gift of life." The fundamental
problem is how the church as a community is to manifest this
new order. Clearly there is to be no violence. There is to be
mutual consideration; husbands are to treat wives with respect.
The voices of women are to be heard in prophecy within the
community; women should be believed in their testimony about
the risen Lord. The texts that speak of submission—a significant
number—seemingly aim to insure the good reputation and good
order of the community. The watchword is found in 1 Corinthians 14:33: "God is not a God of disorder, but of peace." Most of
these texts are looking over the shoulder to see how the community is going to be perceived in the wider world. The writers do
not want the community to be brought into discredit by having
women behaving in ways that are thought to be unseemly.

Cross. The focal image of the cross doesn't apply very well
to many of these texts, but it certainly brings Ephesians 5 sharply

into focus: husbands are called to sacrificial self-giving. They are called to surrender the coercion, domination, and position of superiority that normally would have been theirs in the culture. We might also allude here in passing to the woman who anoints Jesus in Mark 14 as one who perceives the truth that Jesus' identity is to be defined by the cross.

New creation. This image sharply highlights the texts in the third and fourth groups of texts discussed above: In Galatians 3:28, there is no male and female; in Acts 2, in the last days the Spirit is to be poured out on men and women alike; in 1 Corinthians 11:11–12, *nevertheless* in the Lord, men and women are in a relationship of reciprocity. The breaking through of new creation is seen in the story of the Canaanite woman in Matthew 15 who comes and wins over Jesus to extend his grace more widely than he had initially planned. In the sphere of the church, the eschatological promise is to be experienced now. The church is the restored Israel, the city set on a hill where the power of the new creation is breaking into the world. But the "not yet," which I said earlier is part of this new creation image, is also sounded in the household codes. Gender has not been abolished; we still remain men and women as God created us, but something has changed about the way we are to relate to one another. That still doesn't settle what we do, but it shows how the texts fit together into a coherent pattern.

Let's move to the hermeneutical level: what are we to do; how do these texts apply to our lives? Do we have rules here, rules to be applied and obeyed? Yes, we do, most of them restrictive: women are to be silent and be subject, and so on. Do we have principles here? Yes, we do. We have, on the one hand, in 1 Corinthians 11 a principle setting forth a hierarchy in which women are under men; on the other hand, in Galatians 3:28 another principle in which the hierarchy is abolished in the new creation. How are those related to one another? It's a stand-off. What about using paradigms, models, stories? This is where I think it gets interesting. As we look throughout the New Testament at specific stories that are told with female characters, we notice that they tend to be stories about women who lead, take initiative, act in non-traditional roles, assert themselves in surprising ways, and receive grace and blessing because of it. These are stories about "uppity women," and they're all *commended*. None are condemned for getting out of their place. What are we to make of that? We have in the epistles clear models of women—Phoebe, Junia, Prisca—women who are exercising leadership roles in the preaching and mission of the church. So at this level, the New Testament challenges us to open ourselves to the possibilities of new creation.

What about the depiction of symbolic worlds? Here it seems to me we have a collision of two symbolic worlds. On the one hand, we have the orderly household of the pastoral epistles, the world of 1 Timothy 2, where women remain in submission and silence; on the other hand, we have the eschatological, spirit-empowered equality in which women pray, prophesy, preach, and minister in the name of Jesus. Both of these symbolic worlds are present in the New Testament. What are we to do? One more observation about symbolic world is of great interest: when Paul writes, "The man is the head of the woman " (1 Corinthians 11:3), he posits an analogy between God's headship of Christ and the man's headship of the woman. But what happens when we read that analogy in light of a Trinitarian theology, which stresses the unity of God and Christ? What does that do to our picture of what it means to say man is the head of the woman if God is the head of Christ in just the same way? Again, it imaginatively suggests ways of overturning our notions of hierarchy.

If we had more time, I could say more about the relation of the New Testament to other authorities: tradition, reason and experience. But here is the thumbnail sketch: The Christian *tradition* overwhelmingly reinforces patriarchy, although Protestant denominations in the twentieth century have been ordaining women for some time. So the tradition is opening up and suggesting new possibilities, but the tradition dominantly is against women being in authority in the church. *Reason,* in my judgment, basically argues for equality, but it is not unambiguous because there are real differences, as people such as Dave Barry have noted for us. Third, there is the question of *experience.* What does experience teach us about the roles of women and men in the church? You tell me. Once upon a time, I held the view that women shouldn't be in authority in the church because the New Testament taught they should not and that was that. It wasn't until I had the experience of being in a community where women led in worship gracefully and powerfully and were vehicles of God's ministry through the Spirit to the community that I said to myself, "Something is funny here; I had better go back and read more closely." Then I began to read some of these other texts that I have laid out.

This leads us to the final stage of the discernment process that I described as the *pragmatic task*: the embodiment of the Word, putting the Word into practice. It seems to me that what we see happening in the church now, and what we're called to acknowledge and to celebrate and to affirm, is that men and women are being called into forming a new world of relationships, such that we're not boxed in by the world's notions of power and also not boxed in by the world's mechanistic notions of equality. In other words, we do not have to insist that everything is strictly tit-for-tat and that men and women have to do identical things; but we have to recognize that we equally are given gifts to be used in the work of ministry. The goal is mutual servanthood. It seems to me quite clear as we survey this evidence that the New Testament does not give us an unambiguous mandate or a blueprint. We have, on the one hand, subordinationist texts; on the other hand, we have narratives, visions and promises that hold out a new creation of equality and freedom and mutuality for men and women. The funny thing is that God can work and minister grace in either model of community structure, and God has done so in the history of the church.

It seems to me that we now live in a dramatically changed social world, and we are called to fresh discernment. Possibilities exist that did not exist in the first century. In fact, whereas once it may have been regarded as shameful or disorderly to have women in leadership in the first-century community, the reverse may be true now; it may be shameful and disordered for us *not* to have women in leadership. The stories that we have surveyed all too quickly poignantly figure forth a world in which men and women embody the new creation as full partners—or if they do not embody it, at least they prefigure it.

So we have to decide and act. This is my discernment that I offer to you: We are not called to eradicate sexual difference, but to practice mutuality, living into the eschatological future. When we do that, patriarchal and hierarchical understandings of authority are radically transformed by the cross, by the image of Jesus as servant. The point seems obvious once one thinks about it: if the meaning of ordination is servanthood, then why not ordain women? Are women not allowed to be servants? If ordination does *not* mean servanthood, then something has gone terribly wrong. The meaning of ordination then no longer corresponds to Jesus' criteria for leadership. The question we have to ask ourselves is this: How shall we order the life of our community in such a way that we retell the story of God's new creation in Christ, in whom there is no male and female? In order to answer that question faithfully, we must regard our marriages as metaphors, as in Ephesians 5; we must learn new ways of honoring singleness and friendship between men and women; and we must see our life together as women and men in the church as an experimental performance in proress. May it give glory to the one who is the author of the play.

Notes

1. Stephen Barton, *Invitation to the Bible* (London: SPCK, 1997).

2. Ibid., 1–11.

3. Gordon D. Fee, *The First Epistle to the Corinthians.* New International Commentary on the New Testament (Grand Rapids: Eerdmans, 1987).

4. David Schroeder, "Die Haustafeln des Neuen Testaments: Ihre Herkunft und ihr theologischer Sinn" (Th.D. dissertation, University of Hamburg, 1959).

5. Gail O'Day, "Surprised by Faith," *Listening* 24 (1989): 290–301.

Printed in Great Britain
by Amazon